"We want to offer help to those who are separated and embroiled in turmoil, with emotions that seem to be latched onto a roller coaster, with feelings that bounce from terrible lows to unreal highs. And to offer hope to those who are in the realm of post divorce. Moms, dads, kids, even grandparents."

—Anne Claire and H. S. Vigeveno

No One Gets Divorced Alone

How Divorce Affects Moms, Dads, Kids and Grandparents

H.S. Vigeveno & Anne Claire

Regal Books
A Division of GL Publications
Ventura, California, U.S.A.

2017

Published by Regal Books
A Division of GL Publications
Ventura, California 93006
Printed in U.S.A.

Library of Congress Cataloging-in-Publication Data

Vigeveno, H.S.
    No one gets divorced alone.

    1. Divorce—United States—Psychological aspects. 2. Divorced people—United States—Family relationships. 3. Divorce—Religious aspects—Christianity.
    I. Claire, Anne. II. Title.
HQ834.C62   1987   306.8′9   87-9596
ISBN 0-8307-1090-6

Rights for publishing this book in other languages are contracted by Gospel Literature International (GLINT) foundation. GLINT also provides technical help for the adaptation, translation, and publishing of Bible study resources and books in scores of languages worldwide. For further information, contact GLINT, Post Office Box 488, Rosemead, California, 91770, U.S.A., or the publisher.

Dedicated to those who shared their pain
in the hopes that others will have less pain.
And that in their sharing, others will be helped
in finding their way to healing and peace.

DIVORCE
by Ann Doro

Something has wrenched
our memory bank
and torn a family
one from another,
shattering love.
The children cry,
silent.
We are left
holding a handful
of splinters.

Contents

PART IV
Divorce and Remarriage

PART V
Divorce and the Church

Introduction

We want to put our readers at ease. This book does not condemn or judge those who are in the process of separating or who are divorced. Nor is it laden with guilt messages. Throughout the years, we have seen men and women languish in unhappy marriages either broken, or near the point of breaking. They sought separations and then suffered further pain.

Having lived for 21 years with a substance abuser, Marie separated from her husband. "If another one of my Christian friends says to me, 'Have you ever really turned this over to the Lord?' I'm going to scream. Of course I have! I've been a believer since my early 20s. I feel like never returning to that church. They just don't understand."

The frustration and hurt in her words tell us that Marie needed a friend to listen to her, someone to validate her feelings, not a sermonizer. During the despair of separation no one needs a battery of judgments.

The intent and expression of this book is to be there with you, to validate your feelings. We want to offer help to those who are separated and embroiled in turmoil, with emotions that seem to be latched onto a roller coaster, with feelings that bounce from terrible lows to unreal highs. And to offer hope for those who are in the realm of post divorce, moms, dads, kids, even grandparents.

"We got a divorce, me and my mom," Sandra, age 5, explained to her new neighbors. Kids feel divorced too.

Separating parents worry about their children. We often ask, will our kids be OK? Will there be permanent damage?

In the '70s we, the authors, each experienced first-hand the impact of divorce. Anne Claire questioned: "Do all kids react so intensely to divorce? Or are my kids unusually sensitive?" As a Presbyterian minister and former single parent, H. S. Vigeveno was profoundly alarmed by the increase of separating couples who sought counsel in his office and their oft-repeated questions concerning the children.

We came to the conclusion there was a tremendous amount of work and research to be done on the cause and effect of divorce in the family. Concentrating on children, we first interviewed over 100 children and teenagers of all ages as well as parents. After compiling our results, we wrote *Divorce and the Children* (Regal Books, 1979). Since publication we have continued our research. Again and again, we have seen divorce synonymous with pain— pain that travels as a silent, sometimes screaming companion down life's road with us.

Two years ago at a conference a young woman in her early 30s rushed up. She gasped, "Your book! *Divorce and the Children!* It saved my life!" Then she explained. "I had separated from my husband, and while staying with a girlfriend, I planned to commit suicide. My purse was loaded with pills. I went into the guest bedroom carrying your book my friend had just handed me. As a last effort, I flipped pages and began to read the text and Scripture verses. I don't know how to tell you thank you!"

This was more than we had ever dreamed. Shortly after this mother of three small children shared her experience, we pooled our ideas. It was clear there was much more to say about divorce and those affected by it.

In the '80s, as divorce statistics continue to mount, more people need guidance, comfort and encouragement. We are keenly aware there aren't any easy or quick answers. But we have greater empathy, understanding and practical help to offer our readers who face the distressing problems that surround separation, divorce and remarriage.

It is our hope and prayer that this book will prepare and forewarn the vulnerable, the hurting and the unsuspecting. Numerous, uninvited hosts of problems arise as a result of separation, divorce and remarriage.

Today, there is a higher level of awareness. Perhaps people have become more vocal, and situations hidden in the past have been brought to light. We squarely face such matters as sexual abuse and violence in the family, which are far more prevalent than most of us realized in the '70s. We provide single parents with precautions to prevent abuse of their children.

We explore the lives of those who prior to divorce lived in physically as well as emotionally threatening situations. We enter their struggles and conflicts and examine the process of recovery. We learn the importance for the victim to seek help outside the home, *soon* after the abuse occurs.

Together we look at the human tendency to make similar mistakes by ignoring inner feelings. These internal feelings signal when something isn't right. We want to save ourselves from entering relationships that could lead to disastrous second or third marriages. We will also concern ourselves with becoming more sensitive to the Holy Spirit who speaks to us softly and wants to guide us into truth.

Together we take a hard look at *change*. The word slips off our tongues with such ease: change the bed, change the baby, change the tire, change the water in the vase. But *change* within the family structure? Where to live? School? Church? Relatives? Holidays? A birth parent or a stepparent? These are all difficult and traumatic changes for moms, dads and kids.

For all of us, whatever our present situation, it is possible to learn more about ourselves by facing our emotions and recognizing our feelings. We can define issues clearly, learn to understand ourselves and work on solutions. We will meet men and women who have turned their heartaches into success stories. And their stories help us find our way together!

PART I
The Actualities of Divorce

1

Waking up to the Reality of Divorce

In dreams, in visions of the night, when deepest sleep falls upon men, while they sleep on their beds, God makes them listen.
Job 33:15,16, NEB

My ARMS AND MY HANDS were without form, like wax melting. Was I dying? I tried to open my eyes. I struggled to move, but I had no control. Then through a raucous calliope of sound I heard shouting. "Fire! Fire! Twenty minutes to evacuate!"

From the balcony I could see the hungry flames in the canyon. The fire, a twisting turning dragon, was devouring all the brush and trees in its path. My nostrils burned with the scent of smoke; my heart pounded.

Where were my children? And Rob, my husband? I was frozen in terror, unable to move; then the next moment I was spinning like a toy top.

My fingers brushed against the oiled surface of the pecan table. It had been my grandmother's. I had to get it outside!

Somehow the table was on the lawn, and Cindy had helped me. My baby! She's only eight! I couldn't fathom how we managed that alone.

"Are you crazy?" Rob yelled. I could hear him; but where was he?

Dark and distorted, Rob's face appeared in a maze of pain and anxiety. "Come on! We're leaving now!"

"But we have 20 minutes!" I shrieked running across the lawn.

"Wait!" I cried. The station wagon with Rob and my children was headed down the road. "Wait for me!" I screamed at the top of my lungs, but they quickly sped over the rise. I stared in disbelief, crazy with anger as unbearable pain knifed through me.

I wandered back and forth aimlessly along the street, amid a confusing sea of red and yellow trucks and blaring sirens, while firemen struggled to control thick masses of grey white, snake-like hoses.

Then a sense of urgency moved me; I wanted to run. I had to get in the house but my feet were too heavy. Each step took forever, as though I were wading in water.

Inside, through charred rafters, I could see vast stretches of blue sky. I broke into tears, sobs shaking my body. Desperately, I wanted someone to put their arms around me and tell me it was going to be alright again. Then I saw the emerald drapes still neatly pleated, hanging beside the front windows. What a contrast! And my grandmother's hand-painted bone china cups and saucers were sitting on the antique shelves Rob had so carefully refinished.

I laughed out loud suddenly realizing, even though my house didn't have a roof, there was something left to build on. All was not lost!

Then I heard, "Mommie! Mommie! Wake up!" I opened my eyes fully expecting to smell smoke and to see blackened wallpaper. Instead I saw red and pink delicate stripes on a clean white background. The wallpaper wasn't damaged.

I pushed up on my elbows and blinked. "It was only a dream!" I gasped with relief. "Only a dream!"

Sunlight poured into the open window. I sighed and fell back on the pillow taking a deep breath of the fresh morning air, pungent with sage blooming in the canyon.

Cindy had jumped on my bed and was snuggled tightly next to me, her round innocent face turned upward. "Who am I going to live with? You or Daddy?" she asked.

2

Emotions—Friend or Foe?

*Deep calls to deep at the sound of Thy
waterfalls; All Thy breakers and Thy
waves have rolled over me. The LORD will
command His lovingkindness in the
daytime; And His song will be with me in
the night,
A prayer to the God of my life.*
—*Psalm 42:7,8,* NASB

LISA WOKE UP from her dream but not from the reality of agonizing despair. She was suffering from a sense of loss, causing her to lose hope in her world. Lisa had been in almost constant pain since her husband Rob said he was divorcing her. It had come as a terrible shock.

They had argued more and made up less during the past two years. Even earlier Lisa had sensed his withdrawal from her, but when she tried to talk to him about it, he had become sullen and refused to admit anything was wrong between them. She had tried to be understanding and rationalized his actions by convincing herself that men go through stages too. In spite of their lack of communication, she had no idea Rob had been seriously considering divorce.

Not only had Lisa been in a state of despair, she was also caught in a web of self-pity, a monster that whispers lies; lies that said she was no good—that it had been her fault the marriage failed. In response to her negative self-talk, she began to wonder if only she had done this, if only she had done that . . . if only . . . if only . . . then Rob wouldn't have left her and the children.

For months, despair coupled with self-pity kept Lisa from being able to think clearly. But the dream was her turning point and she was spared from slipping from the state of despair into depression.

Lisa related, "Everyone thought we were the ideal Christian family. Then wham—Rob wanted a divorce! I could hardly face my neighbors. I felt my whole world was destroyed. And when the pastor came to see me I couldn't even talk; I was an emotional wreck. I cried and cried.

"But that morning after the dream something happened. I decided I was not going to accept all the blame for the failure of our marriage. Rob had a large part in it too.

"I realized I had been so wrapped up in my unhappiness I hadn't noticed how much the kids were hurting. I became more determined than ever to get my life going forward again. I hated the prospect of being a divorced woman and a single parent, but I had no choice, the papers had been filed, and a court date was assigned."

Recognizing her pain and determined to deal with it, Lisa was able to start a step-by-step process of reclaiming responsibility for her own happiness. She had been happy before; she knew she could be again.

Is Divorce Always Painful?

Does divorce always bring about chaos? Despair? Denial? Depression and anger? When a husband *or* wife first leaves an unhappy marriage, there may be an initial sense of relief, like a heavy burden lifted.

But for most people there is pain. The deep hurt of losing a marriage partner causes emotions to explode. Some react with anger losing self-control, turning love into hatred and violence. They attack others as well as themselves. Some react with paranoia and fear of the unknown.

Others over the years have built strong walls of defense and thick barriers of rationalization. At great length explaining their behavior, they sabotage themselves and frustrate others, rather than acknowledge their feelings and accept their share of the responsibility.

Some become involved in other destructive forms of

denial. Their life philosophy sounds something like this: I will not complain. If I don't pay attention to the knot in my stomach, it will go away. I won't acknowledge frustrations; I'll ignore them. I won't admit I have fears, for if I do, others will think I am weak. Whatever life delivers at my doorstep is mine to take in. I refuse to get angry, but if I feel it, I won't show it. Above all, I will try to be perfect.

After Lisa had gone to several therapy sessions she was able to recognize her denial patterns and was then able to admit Rob had given her signals he wanted out of the marriage, signals she had chosen to ignore.

Denying Feelings

People who want to forget or bury their pain consciously, deliberately deny all forms of discomfort. But our subconscious registers all our emotions. Memory banks never forget. Pain is persistent unless it is acknowledged and dealt with; otherwise it compounds daily, and eventually pays unpleasant dividends.

Others deny feelings in a blatant fashion pretending to be super happy. Their life is one big act. They laugh or joke a great deal, expending vast amounts of energy in boisterous behavior. They mask what they are feeling with a constant state of faked happiness. Their pain can be cloaked in the disguise of humor, but their humor is barbed with sharp tacks that hurt others. Since they aren't honest with themselves, their pain erupts in other forms.

Internalized pain can turn to anger and self-hatred, causing illnesses such as ulcers, colitis or serious allergies.

Have you ever been told when you were disappointed, hurt or angry that you should look at the bright side? Be positive? Maintain a stiff upper lip? Smile, even though you are crying? Take it on the chin? Be a real man, it builds character? Even if you are a woman? These comments attempt to obliterate feelings, as well as reality.

Marie, who was married to a substance abuser for 21 years, tried all of the above. Finally in therapy she realized our Creator made us with feelings, and to deny feelings is to deny how we have been created.

Most of us have a tendency to avoid unpleasantness and rush through anxiety-provoking situations at breakneck speed! We omit the real task of looking at the point of pain, hurt or fear instead of taking our time and identifying our feelings. We need to own our feelings and work through the issues that have caused our discomfort.

If we grew up in a family that suppressed emotion such as joy and anger and were told not to get too happy or not to get angry or not to feel a certain way, then our families were teaching us that our feelings were wrong. The amount of real happiness and contentment we experience in our lives is proportionate to how well we face and handle our pain, hurts, frustrations and anger.

God Created Us with Feelings

We have been created in God's image. He gave us feelings and emotions. And it's OK for us to *feel* feelings. We might be bubbling over with joy or we might be experiencing righteous anger. We may have been treated unfairly, which in turn sets up certain responses. We may feel rejected or gloomy. God has given us an entire range of emotions. It's OK to cry. And it's alright if we're not always brimming over with joy. The Lord God accepts us as we are.

The writer of Ecclesiastes voiced it like this:

There is a right time for everything:
A time to cry . . .
A time to grieve . . .
A time for hating . . .
A time for loving . . .
A time to heal . . .
A time to rebuild (from 3:1-8, *TLB*).

When suffering from a loss such as death, it's normal to experience grief. With a pending divorce, or facing the final decree, it is natural to be in a state of despair. But like grief, the despair may be greater for some people than others. Working through despondency is a process. The cataclysmic event of divorce causes tremendous upheaval to all members within the family structure. If these sudden and stormy changes are not handled properly, they can turn into further disaster with no emergency relief fund in sight.

"I was 12 and we were sitting on the couch. Both of my parents told me they were going to get a divorce. I just ran crying into my room," June said. "I don't want to see my dad. It's really not him personally, but it's what he *did*. I feel sorry for my mom. When my dad calls on the phone, I get in a bad mood and I don't want to talk to him. Most of the time I just hang up on him. Mom never says anything bad about him, but why should I feel an obligation to talk to him or to see him when he didn't feel the responsibility, or whatever, to stay with us?"

For each member of the family, the first and most important step is to get in touch with our feelings. We need to feel the pain, the loss, the grief; own it. We need not condemn ourselves for our feelings. When we are wronged it is normal to feel wronged! We need to be gentle with ourselves and not let anyone, family, friends or the church, lay guilt messages on us!

We need not accept messages such as: *what you should have done* or *ought to do* or even *maybe you deserve this!* And remember there is no set time limit for us to feel better.

There isn't a *right* amount of time to work our way through despair. We can't live out someone else's pattern. Each person is different. But we can be sure of this: If we were a happy person before the divorce we can be again.

A Ray of Hope

Serious-minded and normally conscientious Marc, age 32, had been functioning at a low level, almost in a trance-like state, at work and in his apartment since his wife walked out on him five months before. The care of his seven-year-old son became a concern—a scenario straight out of the classic movie *Kramer vs. Kramer.* Baby-sitters. After school care. How to juggle time between working and the needs of a seven-year-old. How to be a parent and at the same time try to make up for the loss of the other parent who only sees the child occasionally on weekends.

Frequently Marc's son had supper with a playmate down the hall in the same apartment complex. The friend's mother Susan, also a single parent, had often invited Marc to join them. But he couldn't bring himself to accept the invitation because ever since his wife had left, he felt he was a boring person with nothing to offer. As a result of this kind of thinking, his world became dull and bleak looking.

It had been raining off and on in New York City for weeks, causing him to be even more miserable. One bright, brisk and unusually clear afternoon, Marc was riding home from work down First Avenue. In front of the United Nations Building he saw the flags standing straight out in the wind. At the sight of the vividly colored flags, he suddenly felt buoyant and renewed. Gone was the vacuous lack of purpose feeling that had held him captive.

"As soon as I got home," Marc recounted, "I called Susan and asked her out to dinner. She wanted to know whether I had just won the sweepstakes or something!" He couldn't explain to her, or to himself with his usual logic, how for the first time in months he felt hopeful.

Marc joined a mixed therapy group for the recently separated and divorced at his church. His world, which had been toppled by his wife's abrupt departure, eventually turned around for him, but not back to what it had been before. In therapy he learned that you can't view life in logical terms only, but that emotions are legitimate and need to be expressed.

Marc realized it's OK to have fun, something in which he had little practice. By developing better listening skills, Marc slowly began to see the world through the eyes of his son, and in time he discovered the child buried within himself.

Marc became a multi-dimensional person and these changes brought him new confidence. Now he held out the hope that his wife would change her mind about the divorce. He fought fervently against the final divorce proceedings, but she refused to reconsider their marriage. Although Marc suffered keenly from this loss, he was able to ventilate his anger in front of his therapy group, receiving support and appropriate nurturing.

Is it *always* possible to survive trauma, divorce, and change and emerge a more fulfilled person? What if we don't experience a surge of hope? What if there isn't a moment of unexplained buoyancy? What if we lack the energy to catapult ourselves out of the grip of despair? What happens if we slip into a state of depression?

3

"What if I Slip into Depression?"

*Come quickly, Lord, and answer me, for
my depression deepens; don't turn away
from me or I shall die.*
—*Psalm 143:7,* TLB

EVERYONE KNOWS something about depression. There are times when we all experience sadness and gloom, or seem to sink into low places. But depression is unlike despair. Depression is a feeling of inadequacy. Depression is giving up on self. Depression is capitulating to a situation that encircles us. We feel powerless, a loss of control, all of which is accompanied by a definite decrease in activity.

There are mild forms of depression, which means within a few days or weeks we emerge from this low place. However, depression can lead to serious illness if it continues for months.

Then distortions can occur. Sometimes there is difficulty in making decisions and we may lose the ability to concentrate. Depressed people can become extremely sensitive to situations and words that normally wouldn't affect them.

As depression continues, and we are unable to function in our roles, professional services are advisable. *Depression is always treatable*. It can be treated with psychotherapy, psychological or spiritual counseling, drugs under the care of a doctor or a combination of these.

In counseling a person can examine past and present feelings, the times in life where there were troubling experiences, as well as patterns and responses to conflict. Eventually, with effort, the underlying causes for marital discord that brought the traumatic disruption of the marriage are uncovered. It is much better to get help rather than to remain in a continuous state of depression, for depression robs us of vitality, the ability to adapt to change and drastically inhibits personal growth.

Sometimes a supportive member of the family will recognize the symptoms of depression and encourage a person to get help. Randy was able to do this for his mom. While taking a health class in high school he became painfully aware of his mother's depressive condition and gently, but with persistence, insisted she seek help.

Getting Help

In looking back, Rachael, age 36, said, "It was because of Randy's quiet, kind caring that I finally sought counsel. But I became even more discouraged when I was diagnosed as clinically depressed.

"I was paralyzed, both figuratively and literally. Stalled inertia is the most dangerous state in the world. I know, I was there, in bed for days. I only got up to take care of the necessities and then went back to bed. My therapist was trying to help me examine my feelings so I could at least begin to resolve some issues that I had never even acknowledged. But it was too much work. I was so low I was convinced I didn't have any feelings anyway. I was numb. I gave up.

"Tranquilizers, enough for an overdose, were on the nightstand. Then from the back of my head or maybe it was from my soul, I heard something. I'm convinced now it was the voice of God telling me to stay alive. Call it whatever you like, but for me it was the voice of God! He was also telling me to do something to stay alive. The voice kept repeating, *Get up! Get up!* A part of me was extremely resistant. I felt almost safe in my state of depression. I said to myself, I'm depressed and therefore, no one can expect anything from me. I don't have to do anything. And I don't have to take risks. I have this crummy life and I'm in this really crummy mood. I don't have to take a step into the unknown.

"I was slowly killing myself—the end of severe depression. And I knew people died from broken hearts and from lack of nurture and love and I thought I was dying. But the voice said, *LIVE! Put one foot in front of the other and do something!* For me, I had to finally get up and walk around the block. For someone else it could be something significant like walking to the mailbox or riding a bike. Anything! I discovered it didn't have to be a gigantic step. I didn't have to let the world's standard of accomplishments fool me into thinking I had to do something wonderful. Just staying alive was great!

"I had just gone through a divorce and there wasn't anyone to take care of me. I learned to take care of myself. I learned it was OK to feel good, and to be good to myself. I finally figured out I didn't have to feel guilty. It's OK to love myself. Right then being alone was the best thing in the world for me!"

Four years after being diagnosed as clinically depressed, Rachael is still living alone with her children and is sometimes subject to feelings of inadequacy, but she has learned how to manage her low places.

Rachael shared, "When I get stressed out from working and going to college and become paralyzed and depressed, I want to sleep all day. But now I realize that excessive sleep is a form of denial. I encourage myself by saying that if I came through all that has happened and now have the ability to see what I can do and am doing, I'm not going to give up. I'm going to see this one through. Now that I know people can be happy, I'm going to find out what it is all about.

"Yes, I can really sympathize with anyone who is suffering from depression. Even though I can get stressed out and emotionally low I know that I'm not going to slip into serious depression again. I know God worked through my son to get me to a therapist, and at that time I didn't even like God anymore. The last thing I wanted was a therapist who was a Christian! But she was wonderful. She demonstrated love and concern and made it possible for me to have treatment by adjusting the fee to my income, which wasn't much at that time."

The turning point in Rachael's life was when she listened to the voice that said, *Live!*

Furthermore, she is convinced since God helped her overcome depression, He will provide a way out for every person!

God's Promise

In 1 Corinthians 10:13, the apostle Paul says, "Remember this—the wrong desires that come into your life aren't anything new and different. Many others have faced exactly the same problems before you. And no temptation is irresistible. You can trust God to keep the temptation from becoming so strong that you can't stand up against it, for he has promised this and will do what he says. He will show you how to escape temptation's power so that you can bear up patiently against it (*TLB*).

Sin and temptation can be classified as any unhealthy state in which we find ourselves. We can also read *depression* for the word *temptation* in the above verse. God promises to show us a pathway. We can overcome depression!

In the *Amplified Bible,* 1 Corinthians 10:13 reads, "He will [always] also provide the way out—the means of escape to a landing place—that you may be capable and strong and powerful patiently to bear up under it."

This does not mean depression will magically disappear, but it does mean God will provide a way for our escape. The journey may be difficult and beset with obstacles. In the beginning of treatment, Rachael found that examining her feelings was extremely painful. It is hard work to look at inner conflicts and the way we think, in order to get to the place where we can focus on changing behavior and moods.

The way out for some can be found by themselves through Bible study, meditation, reading and independent research. For others the answer comes by reaching out for help in the community. God is unlimited in His ability to help! He works through mental health agencies, clinics, family counseling centers, therapists, counselors, physicians, psychiatrists, ministers, rabbis, priests and members of the laity. Regardless of income, help is available.

Can we arrive at a place of better understanding and become higher functioning, happier, healthier people? Can we survive trauma, divorce and change and emerge as more fulfilled persons? Will we be able to focus in on and help our children deal with the confusing issues divorce has placed at their feet?

4

"No One Told Me I'd Be So Lonely!"

The LORD is righteous in all this ways, unchanging in all that he does; very near to the LORD to those who call to him, who call to him in singleness of heart. He fulfills their desire if only they fear him; he hears their cry and saves them.
—*Psalm 145:17-19,* NEB

BEING SINGLE sure isn't like it used to be," said one recently divorced father.

One of the unexpected surprises of being single, whether a full-time parent or weekend parent, is the gaping loneliness. Having been married, being alone in the evenings, nights and early mornings can be more painful than an operation in the hospital. Even with children around, moments of loneliness pierce the soul like a stabbing needle.

Maybe you don't know what to do with all those mixed up, confused and painful feelings. Perhaps you are even staying late at work to avoid being alone, while the aching fear in your soul whispers, You will always be lonely. Keeping the TV running late into the night and turning it on again first thing in the morning doesn't chase away the gloomy spell of loneliness either.

There are activities to combat aloneness. Which of these have the most appeal to you?

- Attending clubs for singles.
- Going to concerts, plays, movies. With whom? Being alone.
- Doing volunteer work. Joining service organizations.
- Attending a church. Becoming involved in church groups.
- Visiting friends and informing them of your situation.

- Throwing all your energy into your children's activities.
- Learning new skills. Taking adult classes or going to college. Developing new hobbies.
- Joining a mountaineering club: rock climbing or backpacking into the wilderness.
- Joining a nature lover's club and becoming involved in bird-watching and walking.
- Snorkeling and fishing. What about downhill or cross-country skiing.

Any of the above activities and many more can be worthwhile and interesting depending on your individual preference. Yet activities alone can be seductive and deceptive. There is a tendency among singles to throw themselves into activities, thinking that in being busy, one can overcome the feeling of loneliness. It is a delusion.

Elisha, in her late 20s, put it this way: "I joined a ski club. It was fun meeting people and I learned to ski. This was something I had always wanted to do. But finally I admitted to myself as I returned home from a ski weekend and unlocked the door to my apartment, the ache was still there. The fear of being alone forever and the hurts of the past continue to haunt me. Sure it's fun to escape, but when I'm back, I'm still the same empty person. Scared and lonely."

Who Are We?

After a divorce there are twists and turns in the road but also myriads of possibilities and opportunities to meet people. But first there is a need within all of us to find out who we are, what makes us who we are and what causes us to act or react in the manner we do.

Human beings are amazing and complicated. Our brains have a similarity to computers, filled with information and experiences. Everything that has happened to us is neatly filed away in our minds. The good things and the bad.

Situations that threatened our security made deep impressions. Those critical moments from earliest childhood have been permanently recorded, and we are programmed to act and react based on our past in various ways to adversity, conflict, disappointment, failure and crisis. The way we handle our successes and the good things that happen to us have also been filed away in our memories.

This early programming occurred in response to what was being modeled by significant people in our lives. We may have written a counter program in direct opposition to our role models. Perhaps we designed a program that is refined and less destructive than the one that was modeled. Or we might have developed a program based on defiance of authority, unaware of our negativism, sarcasm or self-damaging reactions. The results can be either negative or positive.

In our childhood, faced with an uncomfortable situation, we made decisions either consciously or unconsciously on how we would behave. Often we reacted by observing the manner in which a role model responded to a similar situation. Therefore some of us became carbon copies of our models, perhaps not to our benefit, while others designed and acted out a counter program. In either case we have not emerged as our own persons. Some of us became, in effect, a complex combination of both.

We need to ask ourselves: Are we in charge of our lives or are we following the set patterns from our past? This is a serious and necessary question, and one not quickly answered. When we pursue this question, we may eventually discover who we really are!

Making a Diagnosis

After a divorce it will be most beneficial to do a *mental diagnosis*. A mental diagnosis means spending time, thinking through, reflecting and examining our actions and reactions. A *spiritual diagnosis* takes us even a step further and raises questions about our spiritual nature. If we are Christians we could ask ourselves: Are my actions and reactions in harmony with the teachings of the loving yet confrontive person of Jesus?

Then we can get to work on the real issue before us: Am I being my own person? Or am I in bondage to the past? Jesus, the great liberator, came to this earth to set us free from our past and from our sins, and from the sins of past generations that affect us today!

If we feel we were successful in the majority of our past relationships, we may wonder why it is necessary to change. But if we have failed in marriage, something wasn't working for us; something was wrong. We contributed to the demise of the marriage, even if the other party played a larger role.

Therefore we need to check the computer read-out—the results of our life. After a careful evaluation we must risk taking a significant step, that is, to give ourselves permission to change.

Change is vital to free us from the negativity of the past. Jesus said: "And you will know the truth, and the truth will make you free" (John 8:32, *RSV*). This powerful statement means that Jesus gives us permission to change! He also gives us His Spirit to help facilitate the change. We can write new programs. The capacity for dynamic new input will always be present as long as we are functioning, as long as we are seeking the truth.

In being by ourselves, reflecting and reevaluating isn't enough. The values and the truths Jesus wants us to learn also reach and touch through others. After a divorce we have a need to verbalize the pain, the frustrations of failing in a marriage and all those broken dreams.

Reaching Out for Positive Help

All too often after a divorce a benumbing loneliness sets in. As a result many people are in need of nurturing and are in an extremely vulnerable state. Each of us will do ourselves, as well as our children, a favor if we make it a matter of highest priority to find a group where we can express all of our feelings. We need people who will encourage us to work through our aloneness or other conflicting emotions and issues. We need insight to understand the tapes that play in our heads causing us to behave the way we do.

Finding the right support group is like shopping for a special dress or suit. Sometimes we can't find what we are looking for until we have tried several places. When we locate what might be just right we try it on and look into the mirror. Maybe it's more than we wanted to spend, but it feels and looks so right, we know it will be worth it. The same is true for a group. It's either right for us or it isn't. Sometimes we find it quickly, and other times we may have to check more than one group to find the right one.

The group facilitator or therapist needs to be a confident and knowledgeable person who cares deeply about people. He or she needs to have a track record in working with people, and must provide a climate of confidentiality so we can honestly disclose our deepest feelings. He or she must assist us in discovering who we are and why, as well as being able to work on particular issues and problems, or refer us to someone who can. The group leader needs to be able to guide us in setting attainable goals and help us reach them.

Divorced men and women often are in a tremendous rush to get married again! Our interest in groups, classes and activities spells M-a-r-r-i-a-g-e with a capital *M*. We want to be happy. Right now! We believe erroneously that entering into a new relationship or finding another marriage partner will make us happy. We haven't taken the time to discover the important truth that *no one but ourselves can make us happy and no one is constantly happy.*

During a divorce and for a time thereafter, it's difficult to think straight, to be in touch with our feelings. In this condition we can endanger our future and our children's if we become involved with someone who isn't right for us. All too often many have jumped from the frying pan of loneliness into the fire of a devastating relationship.

This is another reason why a group can be of tremendous value. Obtaining feedback from the group and being held accountable by them is invaluable. Often singles run from place to place seeking pleasure, gratification and thrills to fill up the emptiness in their lives. Failing to find happiness by chasing from relationship to relationship takes its toll. Living in the fast lane is beset with dangers: emotional exhaustion, depression, mental breakdown, physical illness, stress-related diseases, VD or the feared

AIDS (Acquired Immunodeficiency Syndrome). And underneath it all persists the dull pounding ache of loneliness and loss. The people in a group can help us learn to slow down, and they can teach us to listen to ourselves.

Suggesting that we share our hurts and needs, the writer to the Hebrews says, "We ought to see how each of us may best arouse others to love and active goodness, not staying away from our meetings, as some do, but rather encouraging one another" (Heb. 10:24,25, *NEB*).

If you are in the process of overcoming the pain of loneliness, try to answer the following questions about yourself as honestly and as carefully as possible: Do you know who you *really* are? Are you working on becoming your *own* person? Are you *free* from your past?

5

Single and Sexual

*Each one of you must learn to gain
mastery over his body, . . . not giving away
to lust like the pagans.*
—*1 Thessalonians 4:3,4,* NEB

HOW DOES A PERSON who is divorced or separated handle sexual intimacy? Now completely cut off from sexual relations a mountain of new problems arises. The question is often raised but seldom answered.

We have studied Christian literature on the subject and have found very little help. Most often Christian writers assume that since a Christian is not allowed sex outside of marriage, the whole matter is answered. No sex. So there's no necessity for discussion.

For those who are not Christians, there is no commitment to standards. They may believe in moral decency, but today sexual morals are loose and easy. Without commitment to Christ, a person will do what he or she wants.

Too often Christian writers warn the divorcing: If you date a non-Christian there is bound to be a great deal of trouble! A Christian who believes he or she ought to remain celibate sooner or later faces a partner who wants to go to bed on the first or second date, or soon thereafter. Christian counselors offer simple advice: Don't date a non-Christian.

If only the matter could be resolved so easily. The truth is, there are plenty of nominal, single Christians who are not committed to a no-sex-standard. They may profess to be walking with the Lord, but when it comes right down to it, they're looking for sex, intimacy, romance and excitement, just like everyone else. Even after a meeting for singles at church!

What Can Christians Do?

The problem is complicated by the fact that married couples probably entered into a full, warm and giving sexual relationship. Separated, normal sexual relations were cut off. Now they have been brought to a screeching halt! To pretend that this vital, active part of human behavior doesn't matter anymore is, to say the least, extremely unnatural.

The fact is, the more a person attempts to deny a natural function like sex, the more accentuated sex may become mentally. When we don't want to think about something, that very thing is likely to invade our thoughts and take on exaggerated importance!

This leaves Christians open to other ways of fulfilling sexual needs, such as masturbation. Masturbation can turn into compulsive, repetitive, lonely behavior, just when individuals are making a special attempt to avoid relations with the opposite sex. This becomes more disturbing since normal sexual relations have ceased. As a result some Christians are torn apart from personal guilt, a guilt they are unwilling to confess or discuss. Their secret becomes oppressive, and even more compulsive.

Christians may argue that masturbation is not as harmful as committing fornication, but that argument does not resolve the problem of sexual desire.

The subject of masturbation is not touched upon in the Bible. This means it is not a practice that can destroy the soul. On the other hand although it can relieve pent-up sexual tensions, it is selfish in nature and can hardly be considered loving or giving.

For those who love and want to give of themselves, certainly not by going to bed with everyone who makes an invitation, but with the conviction that sex is OK when there is a loving bond, a meaningful relationship is likely to emerge. People feel certain that love is a part of meaningful, sexual relations. Nevertheless, sex outside of marriage is not approved of in Scripture. For those Christians who are aware of the teaching of the Bible, guilt boils below the surface.

What then is a single Christian to do about sexuality?

There are those who point out that if we don't fight our sexuality, but enter into a sexual bond in spite of our guilt, we may feel more relaxed. In this way we may be able to get on with our lives, experience less tension and make better decisions. Others counsel celibacy, but, don't become obsessed with sex-thoughts, they say. When we inordinately need to concentrate on keeping ourselves under control, we may be using up a disproportionate amount of valuable time and energy!

So where does that leave us? Nowhere.

A divorced person, like a widow or widower, faces a major crisis. To dismiss a separation or divorce as if no change has occurred is to do ourselves an injustice. To avoid this crisis by cowardly silence is to expect ourselves to overcome and resolve this new emptiness alone.

If a married person pontificates that sex is sin unless it is blessed of God in marriage, such legalism fails to come to grips with the depth of the problem, and tends to be devoid of empathy. On the other hand, becoming overly empathetic and thereby sanctioning free sexual activity only accumulates guilt before God.

In his book *Bonding: Relationships in the Image of God*[1], Dr. Donald M. Joy points out various stages of contact between people that lead to bonding, or in this case, sexual intimacy. Eye to body is followed by eye to eye.

Then voice to voice, hand to hand, arm to shoulder, arm to waist. Next, face to face, hand to head, hand to body and finally the bonding of one flesh—naked and unashamed. Interpreting "What God has joined together," Dr. Joy states what occurs in one flesh belongs only to intimate marital relations.

When we become aware of these various stages that propel us toward one flesh intimacy, we call a halt to the progression of a relationship. It is easier to say *no* when we are clear about the process and have determined where to stop. As the late D. L. Moody illustrated, when you're in a rowboat at the crest of Niagara Falls there is no way to avoid going over the rapids. So, don't get yourself in that position in the first place! That, of course, is easier said than done. Knowing the limits is one thing; observing them is quite another.

A Single Woman Speaks Out

She is a beautiful, single mom in her early 30s. Taylor talked about sex.

"During and after my divorce I ran around a lot. When I came to a screeching halt I felt sick, depressed and disappointed. First I blamed all the men I had met, then myself.

"It took me a year to get myself mentally, spiritually and physically back together. Then I started going out again. Some men I dated only once or twice. If they wanted to go to bed, and most of them did, I declined. When a particularly attractive man tries to press me into becoming sexually intimate with him, now, I tell him no. The next morning I feel great!

"If he doesn't call me again, I say to myself, 'Well, I didn't mean very much to him. Just another body, another experience.' I've learned the hard way. I'm going to stick to my beliefs. *I feel no guilt. I haven't been used. I'm in charge. I feel good about me!* Maybe someday I'll meet someone who shares my values. I hope so.

"I have girlfriends, both Christians and non-Christians. Some live with guys and others sleep with their boyfriends, but they aren't happy. Most of them dream about marriage, but it seems as if they've given up. Perhaps men would be more interested in marriage if women said *no* to sex outside of marriage and meant it.

"Sex outside of marriage can still spell trouble for us women. We alone have to face the problem of unwanted pregnancy, abortion or a child born out of wedlock. That would be a tough choice for me to make!"

Single women are discovering the avenue of sexual freedom doesn't necessarily lead to the altar.

God is not against sex. He created it. Man didn't invent it. Sex was God's idea! We are God's creation and He knows our frame. He knows our strengths as well as our weaknesses, and we can come to Him in prayer *about everything*.

A Single Man Speaks Out

Harv is in his early 40s. "I didn't want a divorce. I had many reasons. First, our Christian faith, then the kids, everything we have lived for and built together, and then sex. I didn't want to live alone. I knew I couldn't do it. In plain English, I can't live without sex—not for long periods at a time.

"When Nikki told me it was really over, I had to move out. She needed to be with the kids. My apartment was lonely. I wasn't prepared for all this aloneness. It came as a shock. No one was there when I came home, so I kept the TV on in the evenings. I needed company to keep my mind off sex. I had to have noise around me, voices, music.

"Our marriage had been in trouble for a long time, so it didn't take me long to start dating. I haven't always done well. I found out even when I was cautious, some women I went out with expected sex! I was flattered. Women wanted me to sleep with them? That was a whole new ball game. I didn't always want to, but when they are flirtatious and insistent it's hard to resist a beautiful woman. I thought if I didn't, they might think there was something wrong with me—gay or something.

"A Christian life—I guess that means no sex outside of marriage. That's almost impossible for me. If I don't have sex for a long time, I have to do it for myself. I don't like that. It doesn't seem right somehow. But I don't want to play around either.

"After living alone for about nine months I met a fine Christian woman. We've talked about everything, including sex, and we've agreed to wait. I like her. We're talking marriage in the future, but it's too soon. We have some problems to work out, so we're not in a hurry to get married.

"But the sex thing isn't resolved really, just because we've decided to wait. I have lots of feelings. It's tough to feel so much for another and not be able to express it fully. Somehow it doesn't seem quite natural either.

"I really can't be absolutely sure whether we'll get married and when. The other question is, how long can we hold off sexually? We don't want to get married just because we want to sleep together, but how can two people who love each other remain celibate? I don't know about that.

"We've both prayed about it, but we have very strong feelings for each other. We both know what the Bible teaches and we're trying to live by it. So far, so good. But to be honest about it, I don't know how long I can go on like this. Right now, for me it's one day at a time."

Harv's straightforward comments lead to another important consideration. God has created all of us as individuals. Each one of us is unique, different. Some of us have greater trials with our sexual nature than others. God's laws apply to men and women, certainly. His Word stands not only in this world but forever.

The Bible and Sex

The apostle Paul is very clear when he comments on sex outside of marriage (fornication): "This is the will of God . . . you must abstain from fornication; each one of you must learn to gain mastery over his body, to hallow and honour it, not giving way to lust like the pagans who are ignorant of God . . . God called us to holiness . . . . Anyone therefore who flouts these rules is flouting, not man, but God who bestows upon you his Holy Spirit" (1 Thess. 4:3-8, *NEB*).

Since we are uniquely created, we need to understand ourselves, including our sexual nature. For one person continency may be easier than for another. One can become celibate, while another finds celibacy an impossible ideal.

Jesus had something to say about this subject too. Since He was not married, the disciples were very interested and recorded His words on a celibate life: "That is something which not everyone can accept, but only those for whom God has appointed it. For while some are incapable of marriage because they were born so, or were made so by men, there are others who have themselves renounced marriage for the sake of the kingdom of Heaven. Let those accept it who can" (Matt. 19:11,12, *NEB*).

Celibacy became a way of life for the apostle Paul, St. Augustine, St. Francis and others. They had personal conflicts earlier in life, but they were able to commit themselves to sexual continency. Not everyone can live like a saint in *that* sense of the word.

We will never fail when we explore the will and the Word of God. When we discover His will for our lives, we can also ask for the strength and courage to live it out. "Lo, I am with you always, even to the end of the age" (Matt. 28:20, *NASB*) is His word to all who belong to Him, including those who are in the process of divorce.

As individuals it is necessary for us to discover who we are, what we're like, how we're able to survive and live. It is also important to ask:

- What does the Lord expect of me at this time of change in my life?
- What is His will for me?
- How does He want me to respond to His Word?
- How can I live as guilt-free as possible?
- How am I to follow Jesus Christ?
- What does it mean that His Holy Spirit dwells in me?
- Can I draw on His strength, direction and power?

Pursue these questions honestly and fervently.

Believe that the Lord will guide you. But don't expect life to be easy. Jesus does not promise us an easy life. The way He leads us is uphill and narrow, all the way to the Kingdom.

Note:
1. Donald M. Joy, *Bonding: Relationships in the Image of God,* (Waco, TX: Word Books, 1985).

PART II
The Effects of Divorce

6

Children Like the Way
Their Family Was

*You will be happy and it will be
well with you.
Your wife shall be like a fruitful vine,
Within your house,
Your children like olive plants
around your table.*
—*Psalm 128:2,3,* NASB

THE PICTURE of the ideal family as set forth in the Bible presents a happy man with a God-fearing wife and obedient children. The Church has promoted this picture for centuries. Whether we like it or not, it's also the intuitive and heartfelt desire of children. They expect to belong to an ideal family. Children yearn for solidarity. They need to feel attached from a very early age on.

This is what Bart, a young father in his 20s, found out when he visited for the first time after leaving home. Two-year-old Kendra stood by her mom, put her hands on her hips and told him flatly: Go home!

This disturbed Bart tremendously, and he left abruptly. It was weeks before he tried again. The next time wasn't better.

Bart felt sure that Kendra's mother had poisoned his daughter's mind against him. He shared with us that it was like her to hang on to anger and resentment. And because of this he had a mountain to climb. How could he win back the trust of a two-year-old who blamed him for the breakup of her secure home? None of this had ever crossed his mind when he decided to leave his wife. He was really leaving *her*, not Kendra. But this was not how his daughter perceived it. She felt hurt and abandoned.

Whenever five-year-old Meghan comes to visit her father, she treats his fiancée with coldness. Meghan is extremely jealous. She doesn't want Ann near her dad; she wants him all to herself. Only when Ann spends special time with Meghan, baking cookies or fixing her hair, does Meghan seem happier. But it's only temporary. If her father puts his arm around Ann, Meghan makes sure she gets between them right away.

Children and Divorce

What happens inside children's minds when parents divorce? Psychologist Ronald Plotkin says it's hard to tell. Some children become paragons of perfection and attempt to make up for the loss of home. Others become fearful and their mode of behavior reflects their inner fears. They turn hostile, angry, destructive. Others become totally dependent, as if life itself has been drained out of them. But all children of divorce are searching for ways to dispel their confusion, the confusion of having their home destroyed and their foundation broken up.

Specializing with divorced families and students in the fourth through sixth grades of the La Mesa Spring Valley School District in San Diego, Plotkin affirms that very few people are aware of the high anxiety in the children of divorce. This is not a measurable factor since few studies in this area have been done.

The San Diego experiment is modeled after one developed at the University of Rochester in New York by Dr. Joanne Pedro-Carroll. Following a ten-week intensive program of counseling with elementary students, Dr. Pedro-Carroll discovered a significant decrease in withdrawn and acting-out behaviors, decreased learning problems and increased ability to concentrate.

By bringing children together in small groups, children of divorce were more able to tolerate frustration and to demonstrate appropriate assertiveness. They were able to communicate their concerns because they got in touch with their feelings and found acceptance from a neutral person. Initial questionnaires indicated that the children experienced a high degree of anxiety, much higher than parents or teachers thought they had.

The results of the Rochester research will be published and school districts throughout the country have been interested in developing similar programs. According to Dr. Pedro-Carroll, as many as 1 million children are part of separations and divorces each year. At this time only 63 percent of the nation's children live with both of their biological parents. Children of divorce tend to see themselves as different from their peers, but in this program they discover many others who are experiencing the trauma of family breakdowns.

One of the goals of the program is to relieve this sense of isolation. By talking with other children in groups, hope replaces confusion and sadness. Although children, and their parents, may be facing the biggest crises in their lives, they can face these with more confidence.

"When someone dies there is a whole ritual for mourning," submitted Plotkin. "As a divorced parent you don't have that, but you do go through the loss of a dream. With divorce there is little support for the child. Children of divorce have a challenge other children don't have. Some fall or are tripped up. No matter how small or how young they are, they have the human sense of wanting to make sense of things. They want to figure it out."[1]

Coping with Divorce

Dr. Harlen Alcorn, psychologist and family counselor with practices in both California and Colorado, agrees. He told us in an interview:

"This is a loss more severe than death! I would rate divorce as greater grief than death. Number one on the scale. Not many people think of divorce this way. Added to that for Christians is the sense of guilt, of having offended God, of not having lived up to the Christian faith, or failing in something so important as a God-blessed marriage.

"When people say good-bye to one another, this becomes an event. This event leads to a process that has different moods and stages. People are unaware and intolerant of this process. They would like things to come together quickly, not these prolonged moods of mild depression or hurt feelings. Not these continued periods of anger and destructive thinking. Not this feeling like a victim one minute and a villain the next!

"Once you can convince people that divorce is not a quick, easy solution to anything, they can be prepared for these stages. People become terrified that this grief process will go on, that there is no end to it. Even thoughts of vengeance, like, I wish he were dead!, will stop."[2]

According to Dr. Alcorn children go through these same stages and emotions. But because it's held inside more, adults seldom recognize this. They don't understand it. They are too preoccupied with themselves to realize what children of divorce are experiencing. The problems of the children compound the parents' frustrations. A vicious cycle is set in motion: parents worried over their children's behavior only add to their children's confusion.

"They are driving me crazy," said Sally. "Skip is constantly sick and out of school. I have to go to work and I don't like leaving a 9- and 11-year-old at home by themselves. What can I do? When Gordie gets home the two of them fight all the time. I was called in to see the school counselor for the first time because Gordie was causing trouble on the playground."

All of this becomes more complicated for the children because the relationship of the children to the parent is different from the parents to each other. If his mother is hostile, the child may wonder why. Life was not that bad for him when Dad was home. It was great! Dad was lots of fun. Why is he gone? Why aren't Mom and Dad together anymore? Children don't have the capacity to cope with this confusion, not at 3, not at 13.

April, who was 16, was stunned at the news of her parents' separation.

"The day when I came walking downstairs and Mom said, Dad left last night, I just went, Huh? I was in shock. I never thought anything like that would happen. The next day my dad picked me up and talked to me. He said, 'I don't love your mother anymore.' What could I say? He was almost like a stranger to me, saying those strange words. I looked at him and thought, You're Dad? You're the same person who was at our house 24 hours ago watching TV with me? He seemed like somebody else. Then I found out about the other woman. He told Mom about a month later.

"I used to be really down on guys. I didn't trust any of them. I would go out with one and think, You're not going to leave me like my father did. But I'm over that now."

Every anniversary pulls out a memory of the year before. Children are heard to say: This year Daddy's not with us! It's his birthday! Christmas isn't like it used to be.

There are now two sets of families to visit, and in time there may be four sets of grandparents. A child unable to verbalize all these mixed-up feelings may act them out, at 2 years or 12. Small children act out their hostility in aggressiveness with brothers and sisters, or by withdrawing from one or the other of the parents.

Kids tend to blame themselves, and many exhibit regressive behavior, such as fear of the dark and wanting the light left on in their room again. They may even revert to baby talk.

Marilyn talked of her frustrations with her six- and eight-year-olds. "Everything has to be done with them at night, because I have to work now. Sometimes we just sit together. We snuggle on the couch. I can't even give one child my full attention. If one comes to me, the other one hangs around and listens to our conversation. Each one wants me alone, and that's not easy in a small place. They take turns sleeping with me. They just want to be close. And they measure everything—to a teaspoon. They won't let the other get more of Mommy, won't let the other get ahead."

Marilyn helps her children express their fears. "If I were nine years old," she said, "I'd be very sad that my father wasn't home. My daughter is so quiet, and when I said that to her she opened up. Then she began to talk because she felt I understood her."

The Fantasies of Children

Children of divorce are afraid to get angry with their parents for fear the remaining parent may also mysteriously disappear. One parent has left the home. They wonder if the other one will also leave. A parent knows that if he or she gets angry with a child, they are not going to sell them at a swap meet or flush them down the toilet. But the kids don't know that. These fears accelerate pressures in children that no one can realistically withstand.

"Teenagers have a very strong fantasy after divorce. They wish their parents would reunite. They live with this fantasy that at some point in time, Mom and Dad will be back together," stated Mary Ann Lysyk, clinical director of the Boys and Girls Aid Society of San Diego in a recent interview.

"Children don't easily give up their basic desire for the ideal family," she said. "This urgent desire may continue after one or both parents decide to remarry. The youngsters will then do whatever they can to sabotage the possibility of remarriage and drive away potential spouses. When a parent remarries, even *after* remarriage they still want to break it up.

"They may act out this fantasy by becoming difficult to manage. They disobey rules like staying out late at night. They create school problems and have to be brought before the counselor or principal. Some run away from home. They may drift into drugs. Their behavior can become antisocial, even to the point of shoplifting or other crime. These are not conscious problems. Kids don't walk about saying, 'I'm going to hurt my mom or dad.' They just do it."

Lysyk explained how children can affect a marriage. "They assume their natural parent will stick with them no matter how they behave, whereas the stepparent will give up and leave! Now the young person has achieved his or her goal: Mom and Dad will make up and get back together again. That's their underlying agenda. Part of our counsel is to bring all these feelings to the surface, to aid the kids in realizing what is prompting them and then help to change their behavior."

One reason why children and teenagers want their family to be reunited is they're afraid the parent who has custody will divorce them too! When they feel assured this is not likely to happen, by the efforts and concerns of the parent with whom they are living, a new dimension of trust can be built. In effect, in a divorce when one parent leaves, *children have been divorced.* They feel they have been forsaken and, in some cases, abandoned! And this is not their fault at all. The problem lies with the adults' relationship. Children of divorce need help in understanding and accepting the fact.

Much depends on the divorce itself. In a *clean* separation, both husband and wife are aboveboard, remain calm and deal with matters in a straightforward manner. Children accept the truth more readily when parents remain in control of their emotions.

But in a contested divorce that may include hostility, fighting, misunderstanding and the desire to avenge oneself, children of divorce are likely to flounder along for sometime—maybe forever!

Closing the Marriage

When Cameron and Suzy divorced, there was a bitter fight and a great deal of haggling over property. Suzy couldn't give it up. In Suzy's mind, she had been wronged and Cameron was an unreasoning, unfeeling, selfish man.

Seven years later Suzy still seethed with resentment. Their daughter wanted to get married, but Suzy refused to attend the wedding if Cameron was going to give their daughter away. Suzy refused to be in the same room with him. Their daughter loved her parents, and wanted both of them at her wedding.

The daughter finally said to her mother, "Mom, I want you there. I want Dad at my wedding too. You are angry with him, OK. But let it go for a couple of hours. You don't have to sit with him. Just come and be a part of my big day."

Reluctantly, Suzy agreed. She had carried this hostility for seven years and without realizing it, it had connected her to Cameron in spite of their divorce. The marriage had not been properly closed.

A healthy closure of a marriage paves the way for the children to handle the divorce and to face the future with hope. Closure implies anger has been expressed and dealt with and from then on there will be few if any negative remarks made about a former mate. Negative statements only open old wounds and retard emotional growth. Boys tend to be protective of their mothers, but their self-esteem is directly connected to their father. Girls often feel sorry for Daddy because he lives alone in that "awful apartment," but if Dad makes derogatory remarks about his former wife the daughter's self-image is affected, since she identifies with her mother.

Laurie has been able to relegate Vic to a quiet place in her heart. Looking back, Laurie spoke softly, calmly and with fluidity. "My daughter Beverly, six at the time of the divorce, thought her daddy was the best in the world of dads, and grieved the loss greatly. Mike, three, also missed him. Their dad is loving, charming, gregarious, even flamboyant. He is a very nice person. I am grateful I never bad-mouthed him. Through the years I've told my kids the divorce didn't mean their dad didn't love them. It was our problem, not theirs. They have a good relation-ship with him today. Both of the kids now see his limitations, but they love him anyway."

It's not easy for children to be mature when parents are acting like children. Kids get their signals from their parents. Parents are the ones to guide, lead and encourage. Does it seem almost cruel to suggest to a single parent that "Whoever wishes to save his life shall lose it; but whoever loses his life for My sake shall find it" (Matt. 16:25, *NASB*)? When we have been hurt and are in shock we work only to save our own lives, but at some point we need to forget about ourselves and become involved in our children's pain.

Children do not like change. A change in location, friends or school can be very upsetting to children. To remarry may be a gain for an adult, but it's often a loss for the child. Children remember their family the way it was. They are now forced to go along for the ride. If the way is not prepared and their needs are not taken into consideration, nothing but trouble looms ahead.

It is never easy to accept adverse reactions from children and to cope with their rejections. But children must release their pain and express their anger openly. We may serve as the likely target. By becoming that target and accepting those blows, we lose ourselves to find ourselves.

Children may unload on parents and we hope they do express themselves, but it is not appropriate to reveal all the trauma we've been going through to them. We must share our feelings with someone, but not dump our emotions on our children. By unloading on the children we run a risk of making hurtful, harmful and exaggerated statements about their other parent. They can't handle it, and such negative statements do affect them.

One mother confided, "Sometimes it's easier to be unhappy than to face my hurts." It seems easier, but it's not rewarding. To be in charge of ourselves does not imply becoming a stoic who hides his or her humanity. We can be real flesh-and-blood persons with our children. We can tell them we're hurting, but spare them the painful details. Children will accept the truth. If we begin to shade matters and they discover we have lied, their trust in us will fade.

When the apostle Paul said that we were to speak the truth in love (see Eph. 4:15), he was talking about all situations, even those personal relationships that are tested by divorce. We need always to speak the truth in love, no matter how much we feel we've been wronged and no matter how difficult the situation may be.

Children have an idealized picture of the family. They would like Mom and Dad, love and security, happiness and peace—everything in its place. They desire what is familiar and therefore comfortable. We need to remember when children act out their hostilities that they are individuals and need guidance and sympathy in their struggles. They don't need to be yelled at or punished for every misbehavior. But rather parents need to take the time to build a better relationship with each child.

Our children will not turn down compassion, love and care, but we must allow them time to heal. Healing doesn't happen overnight. No one can hurry this process. As we need time, so do they. Parents and children can come through trying periods and quite possibly be closer than ever before.

Concerning our children we need to ask ourselves: What is happening behind the scenes with them? How can we as parents show love and understanding to how the children are feeling on the inside? How can we alleviate some of the pain they are experiencing?

Notes:
1. *Los Angeles Times,* Feb. 18, 1985.
2. Dr. Harlen Alcorn, personal interview with authors.

7

Teenagers Can Help
Themselves

---

*Be happy, young man, while you are
young, and let your heart give you joy in
the days of your youth . . . .
Banish anxiety from your heart and cast
off the troubles of your body . . . .
Remember your Creator in the days
of your youth.*
—*Ecclesiastes 11:9,10; 12:1,* NIV

PARENTS ARE RESPONSIBLE for helping young children, but teenagers must bear some of the burden of recovering from the effects of divorce themselves. We encourage parents to share this book with their teens; then discuss it together.

When Parents Divorce

When divorce occurs, teenagers face difficult, new and sometimes troubled situations, like custody battles, life in a single-parent family, coping with one parent who lives alone or has remarried or has moved to another state. In the near future may loom more problems and the tensions of a step family. Foundations have been shaken. Where is the security of the past now that a family is no longer together?

Perhaps teens don't want to talk to other people about their confused and mixed-up feelings. Their insides feel like scrambled eggs. They wonder if there's someone somewhere who can really understand what they are feeling. Are there others who have survived their parents' divorce? How are *they* doing? The first step to healing is to realize that teens are not out there alone. They have lots of company!

"I felt an emptiness inside, like something was taken

away from me," shared Art. "I felt it was my fault the divorce happened. Then I asked my brothers, and they felt that way too. I went through a lot of turmoil at 14. I got in with a wild crowd. I skipped classes. My grades went down. That was because I had problems at home. They were the worst years I ever had."

Millie is now 19. Her parents divorced when she was a senior in high school, but the family discord had been severe for at least five years.

"The marriage wasn't very good. It made me feel like I didn't even want to be around. They were either fighting all the time or not speaking to each other. One night I really got upset and left. That's the worst thing I can remember. I just left for a few hours, not overnight or anything. You always hear about other people being divorced, but you don't think about your own parents. Like my friends would say, 'Your parents are getting a divorce?' I'd say, 'Yes.' They'd say, 'That's too bad.' No, it isn't really. It's not that bad. After some time I really thought it was for the best—no more fighting and arguing. But at first I was upset and confused."

"My parents had been married almost 25 years," submitted Sherry, who was in her late teens. "I blamed myself a lot, but I didn't know why I blamed myself. They went through two other kids without divorcing, and then here comes me, and they get a divorce! I felt guilty. Maybe I still do a little. It's hard to live through the ages of 13, 14 and 15. That's a really self-incriminating age anyway, and then to have a divorce? For me it shook up everything that I believed in. The more difficult I became, fighting with Mom all the time, the more guilty I felt."

Each divorce is different. A teenager living with a father may have to handle a weeping mother on the phone.

Another, living with a mother, has to cope with a father who suddenly wants to lavish expensive gifts on them. How can teens help their moms work through their frustrations when they can hardly keep from crying themselves? How do they behave when they're invited to dinner with their dad and his new girlfriend?

"For 20 years my father had been an elder in the church," related Ernie. "Then he left Mom and moved in with another woman. He met this woman through the church. Mom says I am the only one she can depend on now, since I'm the youngest. It's just too much! I can't tell her what to do, even though I'm almost 18."

"It would have been better if he had died," Charlie blurted out about his father, who left the family abruptly. "I'm so disappointed. I miss him so much. Why did he desert me like this?"

"It's not fair. I want a family like everyone else," added Stephanie, a collegiate whose parents broke up when she went off to college. It shocked her and left her devastated, even though she was living away from home. It seemed to Stephanie that part of her once secure world had collapsed like a washed-out bridge.

The teen's world has fallen apart when their parents divorce, and they find it hard to understand why their father and mother can no longer live together. Of course they are angry about it, disturbed and confused, beginning to feel hostile and rejected. Perhaps even guilty! They may wonder if some of the troubles their parents had were their fault. Furthermore, they may be wondering what will happen to them now. What is in their future? Where will they live? They're full of questions they may be too afraid to ask.

Experiencing turmoil is normal. What can they do

about it? They can begin by accepting their feelings. One way to be able to sort out the issues they are facing is to sit down and talk with someone they can trust. Someone who will make every effort to understand and bring helpful guidance and insight.

"I was upset being away from my father," Vera spoke emotionally. "More than anything I was ashamed! Ashamed of living in that crummy place, and ashamed of my parents for splitting up. I didn't tell a soul. One day in class I broke down. The teacher kept me after class and I told him why I was feeling so upset. He became my confidant. Then I found out he was a Christian. We talked about lots of things—my life, my mom and dad, school and God too. Every day I went to see him. He took a real interest in me. If he hadn't been there, I don't know what I might have done."

In time perhaps the parent the teen is living with will be able to help him share his feelings, and possibly so will the parent whom he visits. This will depend on each individual, of course. Perhaps both of them will be able to listen and help. As they are able to overcome their own pain, they will be more free to speak openly with their children.

Ted's father talked about his loneliness. He felt lonely in an empty house. He felt inadequate to help his son.

"Ted's mother moved out and Ted Jr. is with me part of the time. I'm very lonely and have nothing to do. I have no social activity. Nothing to fill up my evenings. TV gets boring. Ted sees me suffering and I know I convey my emptiness to him. He asks me questions, but I don't answer them very well. I should because I am a counselor. But I don't have myself together. Before my separation I had a reason for doing what I was doing—for my family, for my life. My work was meaningful. Now the bottom has dropped out of everything and I have to find new reasons for living."

It bothered Ted because he felt helpless with his son. He could counsel others but not his own son.

"I understand why some men run out on their families," Ted's dad continued. "They refuse to pay child support, and run away to start all over in another state, because they have lost purpose and meaning. It is a humbling experience to fail in something as big as marriage. I am really brought low. It's painful for me to admit after so many years that I have failed."

Ted wanted to guide his son, but he himself was hurting so much. It took a year of working hard at their relationship before Ted could help him. Now father and son talk honestly and openly with each other. It takes time, but it's obvious adults struggle also.

Teens need to allow their emotions to surface; find someone to talk to about them. Once they understand why they feel the way they do and accept their right to feel this way, they will be able to begin to face the change that's going on in their lives.

Teenagers Blame Themselves

Many times teens believe that if only they had been easier to get along with or behaved more like their parents wanted them to, the separation would not have occurred.

This tendency to take the blame is natural. Brothers and sisters fight. Often this fighting contributes to the unrest in a home and upsets their parents. Some parents disagree about ways to discipline or control their children. These are normal growing-up pangs in many families. But if one parent says, "If only you had behaved better we would not have split up," they are dumping their own guilt in the wrong place.

Teens should not accept this guilt! It doesn't belong to them. Parents are accountable for their own actions. Teens are not responsible for their parents' marriage. As adults, parents need to assume responsibility for their own lives. Parents do not separate because of their children. They divorce because one or both of them made the decision to divorce.

If teens continue to blame themselves, they need to hand over their feelings of guilt to the Lord. They can ask Him to take their burden. They need to pray and believe the good news. The good news that Jesus Christ offers complete forgiveness for all our guilt. Jesus died for our sins. Jesus invites everyone to come to Him. Everyone is welcome, no matter what they have done or how they feel. At the place where we hurt the most, we can experience the good news of being made well. Look up such verses as Matthew 11:28-30, John 6:37, Romans 5:20 and 1 John 1:9, and read what the good news can mean to each of us.

Handling Anger

"Don't take sides like I did," Kay, 16, stated. "I was so angry in the beginning I didn't want to see my dad. He used to write me; I didn't answer. For about a year I didn't see him or even talk to him on the phone. When the divorce was over and he got married, and this was the way life was going to be, then I was able to see him. He asked me to his wedding, but I didn't go. I told him I couldn't handle that. I used to throw things, but I don't any more. I grew out of that, finally."

When we believe someone has let us down, it's only natural to feel anger. If you are a teen reading this, is that how you feel about one or maybe both of your parents? You don't know why, but you may want to get even for all the hurt you're experiencing. This is why some kids upset the home, others become problems at school and run with the wrong crowd.

The first thing you will need to do is come to terms with your anger. Admit you are angry, but don't retaliate or try to make the problem worse. Revenge strikes out at the other person, but it lashes back and destroys something good in you. If both your parents want to spend time with you, don't refuse their offer. Your parent who lives alone is very lonely. Often parents don't look ahead or think about the loneliness they will face when they move out of the house. They don't see ahead of time the heartaches and pain, sense of failure or depression.

Teens may believe their parents deserve to feel this way. Maybe they do. Maybe they don't. But parents can do without their children's wrath. Life is already very difficult for them. So talk to them. Tell them how you really feel. Honesty will produce a healing.

Don't go into your room, shut the door and keep to yourself. You need space, but hiding is not healthy. Whenever you push your feelings deep inside, you will become more depressed and start to feel sorry for yourself. That can be like riding a merry-go-round going nowhere. You will find yourself thinking only about your problems and they can grow into mountains. You don't need that. So get out of your room. Start circulating.

Joe was coming apart. At 19 he couldn't handle the breakup of his family. Joe and his mother had a special relationship.

"She was my best friend," he said of his warm and responsive mom. "I'm really sick because of her, and I can't handle it," he admitted.

Joe's mother at 42 secretly started dating a man 16 years her senior. When she admitted the affair to her husband, she did it with malice and revenge. She had long nursed a resentment toward her husband for his infidelity 10 years earlier. She never forgave Joe's father. Now she insisted on a divorce, saying she was in love with the older man.

Joe was unable to handle his parents' problems, so he went to live with his grandmother. His younger sister cried a lot in her room, and Joe wanted to help, but he didn't know how.

Living with his grandmother didn't resolve anything for Joe, because he withdrew even more until his grandmother was able to get him to her church. She introduced him to some young people and he accepted their friendship. Joe found they believed in Jesus Christ and took their faith seriously. They were fun to be around. They helped Joe to come out of himself and face life.

Look for Positive Help

Going to other people for comfort and acceptance is a step in the right direction, but be careful *to whom* you turn. When you're hurting you are very vulnerable. Look for people with good morals who enjoy life and have good values. The wrong crowd can easily influence someone who is going through a crisis and is in a vulnerable condition.

There will always be people who will gladly introduce you to their life-style and habits—drugs, drinking, smoking, sexual freedom. Once you start a habit it's very hard to break it. It's always easier not to start than to have to stop! Teenagers often turn to sex for feeling accepted. Remember you are vulnerable. You are hurting. You want to be accepted by someone. Anyone. It's not wrong to want acceptance, but recognize the danger signals. Participating with those people who include anyone who joins them in their lesser life-style isn't acceptance at all!

The clinical psychologist, Mary Ann Lysyk, discussed with us how some young people have overcome the destructive habits in their lives.

"Insight can produce change! That's why we bring kids together in small groups where they can talk with one another. In these groups kids are given the opportunity to discuss their feelings and their erratic behavior. Then someone else in the group relates to those feelings. They talk about their own pain and hurt. The teenager experiences acceptance and this acceptance spreads to the others. The group begins to look for other ways of handling their problems.

"When kids trust the group, they get some of those mixed-up feelings out into the open. They support one another. They pinpoint their pain and all the emotions around it. It then becomes OK to put it away, to be done with it. I've seen that happen again and again, like a great big burden lifted from their shoulders.

"Sometimes kids won't talk about the real issues, because if they say it, *it's real.* They don't want to admit the reality of their feelings. They want their way out behavior to be more of a fantasy. Living in a fantasy world with drugs or the wrong crowd makes them forget. But the pain is still there. Once they're able to talk about it, it's no longer a fantasy. Then it's real! And healing can take place when the hurt is no longer held inside."

Looking Back

Liz is 21. She spoke with maturity about the divorce that took place in her family when she was 15.

"It never crossed my mind that my parents would split! This divorce really shook me up, you know. It came at a bad time. It never would have been a good time, but maybe younger I would have adjusted better. Maybe older I would have understood more. At 13 and 14 I already felt I was the ugliest person in the world, so insecure. And then, to have that happen it just kept me at that age emotionally until I was 20. Then I worked through analysis with a counselor. I learned I was emotionally stuck at 13 and 14. This was and is the most traumatic thing that ever happened in my whole life! Counseling helped me to understand myself. I just couldn't say the word *divorce*. The counselor made me say it over and over until I was letting the things that were inside me pour out. It was incredible. So many things I felt angry about! I just had never told anyone, not my mother or my dad. All this anger was destroying me."

Liz talked about helping other kids who are going through a family crisis.

"Knowing what I know now, I would demand more honesty from my parents. Make them talk to you rather than you doing some juvenile act to gain their attention. You have rights too. Tell them you want to know straight on what is happening. You don't have to know all their sexual problems. Ask, 'Where do I fit in?' I never demanded that. My parents set themselves up as model parents. They didn't tell anyone about their problems, and that's not fair. But love your parents, because they're going through a lot of emotional stress.

"Sometimes people say that if parents get divorced, so will their children after they marry. Maybe. But I think that you can learn from your experiences. I've got the desire to succeed where my parents didn't. Before I enter into a marriage and have kids, I'll have to think hard."

Others have expressed similar ideas.

"Divorce has made me more careful. I don't want someone who fits into the image of my father," commented Alice. "I want a marriage where divorce is not going to be an option."

"I've thought about marriage," Shirly added seriously. "I think I'll have to marry a Christian. When I date a Christian guy I find that he is much nicer, more considerate, loving and tender. In the past the guys I dated were turkeys. With a Christian guy I have something in common. We both believe in the Lord and have similar values. We talk the same language."

Melody spoke from a backdrop of child abuse. "When I get married and have kids I'm not going to get divorced because, well, first of all, I'm not going to get married unless I know it's going to last and I'm really sure of myself. And I wouldn't get divorced until the kids have moved out, because it's not fair for the kids to suffer. Unless they ask me to, and say it's too awful living like this. One thing I'm going to make sure of—no violence! I can tell just by looking at a person, by how he acts, if he is violent. They may not think it shows, but I know by the way a person is. I have a boyfriend and he treats me good."

Teenagers from divorced families ponder future relationships because of family troubles. They raise questions and think through the man-woman relationship, something they might not have done otherwise. The rude interruption of divorce brings about an awakening. They learn to ask questions about life. They become more aware of their feelings, more aware of relationships. They discover God can bring something *good* out of a *bad* situation!

The Bible makes that point many times. Our trials have value. They prepare us for the future. "We know that in all things God works for the good of those who love him, who have been called according to his purpose" (Rom. 8:28, *NIV*).

Perhaps the most valuable information we can offer teens as they begin the process of healing is:

One. Find someone with whom you can share your thoughts and feelings.

Two. Ask God for help and guidance.

Three. Take charge of yourself.

Four. Talk to your parents honestly about your feelings.

Five. Be patient—God works for the good of those who love Him.

8

Grandparents in Crisis

*The LORD is near to all who
call upon Him.*
—Psalm 145:18, NASB

SOFT, CUDDLY AND PINK, a beautiful baby girl, and I couldn't wait to hold her!" Dianne described her thoughts as she gazed at her first grandchild through the nursery window.

"Then there were more. Our son Clarence and his wife Lorelei had three children, each adorable and unique. They lived nearby and we saw them often. The grandchildren became the center of our existence. Barry, my husband, now retired, had spent little time with our children when they were young, however, he enjoyed watching the growth of our grandchildren. Being grandparents brought us great joy!

"But late one afternoon Clarence dropped a bomb. He was filing for divorce. *Divorce?* We went into shock. Questions and comments tumbled from our lips.

"'I can't believe you and Lorelei would divorce!' I cried. 'You come from a heritage of Christians who work things out. Are you a quitter? We are not quitters!

"'Did you have counseling?' Barry queried. 'You'll get counseling, of course! What about the kids?' Clarence left in a huff, angry with both of us.

"Never before or since have I experienced such anguish. Our family wasn't immune to the divorce epidemic! The despair in our household hovered like a clammy fog. Barry and I asked each other over and over what went wrong? We didn't have any answers, just the feeling that maybe there was something we could have done to have prevented this calamity.

"For months friends tried to comfort me; others seemed embarrassed when I cried. We found many of our Christian friends were not clear on their views of divorce. Barry and I had always held tenaciously to the position that divorce was not an option for Christians. We believed that those out of fellowship with Christ divorced, and if one were in Christ, difficulties could be worked out. We were forced to rethink our beliefs and in doing so, we realized we had been very judgmental and unrealistic."

Grandparents Want to Be Supportive

Parents desire the best for their adult children and their grandchildren. Their willingness to help comes from love. Sometimes in addition to love it also stems from feeling out of control. Grandparents are not the decision makers. They don't set family policy outside their walls. They see and feel the effects of the separation on all family members including themselves, and in essence, would like to set everything in order.

They also feel guilty because they didn't role model the *perfect marriage*. Guilt may cause them to think *if only* we had done a better job as parents, this divorce wouldn't be happening. They want their pain, their adult children's separation and the confusion of the grandchildren to be eradicated immediately! Then with good intentions and reacting from a combination of love, guilt and fear, they often rush in with patch kits, hoping to fix the deep wounds. While making various suggestions, they may liberally sprinkle their conversations with Bible verses, sometimes unfortunately causing alienation rather than providing the intended comfort.

Dianne and Barry discovered this the hard way. Their

son and daughter-in-law were offended by their suggestions. Hostility grew. As a result the grandparents were
seldom allowed to see the grandchildren, causing additional pain for both Dianne and Barry. To cope with the
loss in his life, Barry doubled the amount of time he was
spending on the golf course. Dianne chose to go to a counselor because of her daughter-in-law's icy suggestion that
she needed it. Dianne thought Lorelei was the one to go!
But in counseling, Dianne made the significant discovery
that she needed to disconnect from her grown son.

After about a year, relationships have resumed
between the grandparents and both divorced parents.
Lorelei, who has custody of the children, has been able to
forgive Dianne and Barry for what she felt were attempts
to control her. The grandchildren are again allowed to visit
their grandparents and enjoy weekend sleep-overs, much
the same as it had been before the separation.

When their son Clarence married a second time,
Dianne said their household became the scene of a balanc-
ing act. The grandparents are doing their best to keep
relationships clear of obstacles as they seek to include a
new daughter-in-law, and continue to work on a friendly,
open relationship with Lorelei.

Clarence and his second wife now have a baby. "With
these two families, we are constantly reminded of our
need to be sensitive to everyone. Sometimes it's like
walking on thin ice. Our grandchildren bring us an incredible amount of joy. Barry is again registering the children's
growth on a wall in the garage."

Handling the Pain

How can grandparents handle the triple dose of pain—

theirs, their adult children's and grandchildren's? One grandmother in her 40s mused, "I thought all the heartaches and troubles of parenthood were over when my daughter left on her honeymoon. It wasn't until after her divorce that I understood being a parent *is* forever and so is being a grandparent! I hurt when each of them hurt."

Dianne offers these suggestions. "Try not to back away from the pain. Trust the Lord for His guidance. His Word gives assurance He will be with us; and we can grow spiritually and emotionally through suffering, even though at the time I was the first to admit it didn't seem likely! I really struggled. I even felt deserted when Barry spent so much time on the golf course. I resented his free time.

"In counseling I realized he needed the space. This was his way of working through his feelings. He said he gained strength from being outdoors. It reminded him that God is in control; especially when it rained and he couldn't play golf! On those dark days he seemed moody and silent, but God was dealing with him. Barry realized he had been compensating. He tried to be the parent to his grandchildren he had failed to be to his own.

Not everyone can work through conflict and turmoil alone with God, as Barry did. Dianne needed people to minister to her and benefited from counseling. As a result both Dianne and Barry have increased their faith in God and testify to His promises.

"God doesn't make troubles go away when we ask," Barry said. "Instead He promises to be with us in our trials."

Passages

After interviewing grandparents from various walks of

life who have survived fragmented families, we find a similar thread weaves through many situations. At the onset there is shock, an upheaval that stirs our emotions unlike other crises. This unsettling creates unrest and fear. Even if the divorce occurred as a result of abuse, and relief springs from the termination of unfair treatment, the transition is beset with highs and lows due to the changes in the family structure.

Grandparents worry about their grown children and what will happen to their grandchildren. Being older and wiser, they are often fearful of rifts that can create permanent damage in the extended family. Divorce is like a rock heaved into a quiet pond, creating ripples that sweep into ever-widening circles. Divorce sets reactions into sometimes endless motion.

Guidelines for Grandparents

The following suggestions are guidelines for grandparents to help maintain relationships with their adult children, grandchildren and other family members during separation and divorce.

One. The initial stage of separation is the most unstable period. This is the time for grandparents to comfort each other with thoughts from the Bible. By daily focusing on a verse or two, firm ground will be established with the Lord. He promises to sustain us in troubled and fearful times. The following verses are good to memorize:

> Casting all your anxiety upon Him, because He cares for you (1 Pet. 5:7, *NASB*). GOD is our refuge and strength, A very present help in trouble (Ps. 46:1, *NASB*). The LORD is near to

all who call upon Him, To all who call upon Him
in truth (Ps. 145:18, *NASB*).

Two. After the initial shock, listen. Try not to offer
advice, don't be critical or ask questions that smack of
judgment (easier said than done).

Often, words are spoken only to be regretted later. As
the recently separated unload on you, try not to take sides
or defend either party. Taking sides causes further alienation. Listen for feelings. Validate them. Small children
express their feelings, too. Listen with empathy. You will
demonstrate you care by sympathetic reflections and your
willingness to hear. They all need you as a sounding board
for their feelings, not yours.

> Claim verses like Psalm 141:1-3:
> O LORD, I call upon Thee; hasten to me!
> Give ear to my voice when I call to Thee!
> May my prayer be counted as incense before
> Thee;
> The lifting up of my hands as the evening offer-
> ing.
> Set a guard, O LORD, over my mouth;
> Keep watch over the door of my lips (*NASB*).

Three. As soon as possible renew the normal ebb and
flow of your daily life. This is not the time to stop your fit-
ness program whether it's jogging, aerobics, walking,
bicycling, etc. Exercise helps to ease tensions from emotionally fatigued bodies. If you have not been in the habit of
regular exercise, begin to enjoy long leisurely walks with
your spouse.

Four. More than likely you will work through stages.

There may be days when you are sad or depressed, then possibly hopeful feelings will bubble forth. The least bit of encouraging news can create mood swings because you're clinging to the hope of reconciliation. Your grandchildren's faces reflect the turmoil they are feeling. You see they are difficult to manage because they are acting out their hurts and fears; some younger children may resume bedwetting, and older children may engage in open rebellion. You long for more peaceful days and wish there was something you could do to affect a healthy reunion.

Five. You will feel anger. You are angry with your son or daughter, your son-in-law or daughter-in-law, or their parents. If *they* had only raised their children right, your family wouldn't be in this difficult, painful situation today! You may even want to reach for the phone and tell the other grandparents a thing or two. Maybe you are smarting from pain because they blame you!

Six. Find someone neutral with whom you can share your feelings. Perhaps a close friend or your minister. Find someone who will *hear* you and *validate* your pain and *listen* to you. If you do not get relief, you may consider short-term therapy. This could be particularly helpful if you have experienced a divorce, or a significant loss as a child or adult, and have not worked through the trial. Perhaps there are issues you have not dealt with. You could be experiencing additional grief stemming from re-opened tender spots that have not healed.

Seven. Watch out for negative self-talk that begins with, "if only" and "what if." You did your best raising your son or daughter. Blaming yourself for their separation is a self-defeating message. You may feel guilty. Loving, concerned people feel guilty because they care. But the separated couple lives in the real world just like you do. They are entitled to make mistakes and learn as you have. Try not to add fuel to their emotional fire, nor your own. This is the time to be meek, prayerful and place confidence in the Lord. Parenting days are over. Your children are adults now. Comfort yourself with the truth that where the Lord has begun a good work He promises to bring it to fruition (see Phil. 1:6).

Eight. What if your daughter or son or a son- or daughter-in-law comes to you for advice? Can you give sound advice when your insides are jumbled? Would it be possible for you to share your feelings that you hurt too, and suggest they find a professional counselor? If it is difficult to be objective even though you may be a professional, perhaps it would be better to have another party provide counsel.

Nine. If you are approached for tangible help, before giving financial aid, talk it over very carefully. If a separated party wants to live with you or wants you to take the grandchildren for an indefinite period, move slowly. Give yourself time. Few decisions need to be made immediately. If you are a single grandparent, discuss the proposal with a clear-thinking individual who knows your family. Go slowly with what could alter your life-style—you have finished raising children! If you decide to make a commitment of money, housing or time such as daily childcare, set a future date to re-evaluate the situation. Try to make arrangements that have a tentative date for termination.

Single parents will find freedom without responsibility, when grandparents shoulder more than their share of the load or become overprotective. You could be blocking a parent from learning how to cope with difficult times and develop his or her strengths. Resentment can creep in causing friction between the grandparents and the parent.

94 No One Gets Divorced Alone

This friction places grandchildren at additional risk by the creation of more conflict.

Ten. Grandparents have a common, often unexpressed fear that following a divorce settlement they will not be able to see their grandchildren. In most states grandparents have the right to obtain custody if the natural parents are unable to be providers and caretakers. But what if a natural parent moves or secrets the children away? What about visitation rights for grandparents? Because of litigation and persistence on the part of grandparents who were denied the right to see their grandchildren, changes have been made in Family Law in many states. In the event of death, separation or divorce, grandparents have the right to petition the courts for visitation. The courts could *award visitation to grandparents* upon a showing that such visitation is in the child's best interest.

Even with the changes in Family Law, one Christian couple decided against taking legal action. Their grandson is now 15. They only saw him a few times as an infant. After an early divorce, their young daughter-in-law secreted the child away slipping from state to state. His father also lost track of them. The grandparents know their grandson's address now, but his mother still doesn't want her son to have a relationship with the grandparents.

After much prayer the grandparents said, "We feel confident that when he is 18, he'll come looking for us and the other members of our family." If grandchildren are moved away and hidden without cause, seeking counsel from an attorney could be helpful. Grandparents' visitation schedules could be written into the divorce agreement. However, legally pursuing visitation rights for grandparents needs to be thought through carefully. In most cases, after frayed emotions settle there may not be a problem.

Grandparents' rights could be viewed as a back-up plan.

Eleven. Grandparents can also seek counsel from mediators in conciliation courts. There are mediators who welcome extended family members in discussions concerning custody and visitation arrangements. A mediator in Los Angeles held in high regard by co-workers and members of the bench and bar welcomes grandparents, other family members, and even neighbors; all who are interested in the well-being of the children and who want to be part of their network of support. She feels the more people who engage in open communication, the better it will be for the children and their parents.

Twelve. There are grandparents who become the caretakers of children, whether by court-awarded custody, or by private temporary arrangement. For years grandparents have lovingly fulfilled their permanent or temporary role as *parents.* Today there is more emotional help and support in the community for grandparents. Low cost grandparents' groups in family clinics (check churches, also) span the country. There, grandparents meet weekly with a group facilitator while the children participate in a kid's therapy group.

Thirteen. Grandchildren of divorce also have special issues. A child may be acting out in anger that stems from feeling rejected. Children often feel abandoned by their parents, even though they may be receiving excellent care from grandparents. In our society it is not unusual to have a natural parent in a rehabilitation hospital overcoming addiction to a mind-altering substance. This is not only occurring in the secular world, but also in the Christian world. As Christians we need to face the issues and accept responsibility, not to judge or deny the problem's existence. Those who struggle with addictions need our love, concern and support. While the parent is in such a program, visitation could be arranged for the child to continue the connection with the parent.

Frequently children living with a grandparent will gravitate to a play telephone and pretend to be talking to their mother or father, carrying on animated conversations. Sometimes a child will hold the phone tightly to his ear, listening and nodding his head. Sometimes a child will slam the phone down in anger. Even angry children crave contact with absent parents.

Though grandparents provide love, food, shelter, and fill in extras by reading, listening to prayers and taking grandchildren on outings, they are not a replacement for natural parents. Children need to be told, to the level of their emotional understanding and maturity, the truth about their parents. They also need assurance that their parents love them and can't take care of them at this time. Because of their love, parents have provided a home for their children with their grandmother and grandfather, until they (the parent) can again accept responsibility.

Fourteen. A goal may very well be reunion with the natural parent. When the goal is reached the special care a grandparent has provided will end. Reunification creates another change, a period of adjustment for the children, parents and grandparents. If the grandparenting-parenting period was fulfilling it may be difficult to give up the responsibility. Should it be painful to disconnect from the grandchildren, and a grandparent becomes unduly depressed, therapy could help to transform the energy expended in grandparenting to another source of service and personal fulfillment.

Grandparents who help out in times of crisis receive a blessing, and are a blessing to the separating family. But grandparents can't always meet every need, and not all sons and daughters and sons- and daughters-in-law desire or accept their help. Grandparents are often faced with limitations, but that doesn't hinder them from praying for their grandchildren. The Lord works in strange and mysterious ways. Whatever the situation, it is well to leave it in the Lord's hands. Trust is an attitude that can heal wounds and feelings.

PART III
The Issues of Divorce

9

"Who Am I Going to Live With?"

Yet those who wait for the LORD
Will gain new strength;
They will mount up with wings like eagles,
They will run and not get tired,
They will walk and not become weary.
—*Isaiah 40:31*, NASB

WHO AM I GOING TO LIVE WITH?" Cindy, Lisa's eight-year-old daughter's question raised in chapter one joins in chorus with countless other children.

The ideal answer to the child of divorce would be, both parents. "Mom and Dad will nurture you, love you and both of us will take care of you. You will live in the home that each of us have separately provided. We promise to always be there for you until someday like an eagle, on your own strength, you will fly away."

The optimal situation for the child of divorce is *joint parenthood,* i.e., both parents cooperating with each other and considering what is best for the child. The child then benefits immeasurably by having paternal as well as maternal care. Divorce need not cancel either parent's rights or responsibilities to the child. The child required both Mom and Dad before the divorce. The universal need for both parents has not disappeared.

Before the separation, some parents attempt to mask their problems by fighting silently through passive aggression creating an undercurrent of hostility and tension. Others engage in verbal battles creating a warlike atmosphere. Parents may very well enjoy a sense of relief now that a separation has taken place. The household from their point of view has been transformed into a peaceful haven.

But the child does not embrace the change. The child

feels the loss of the absent parent keenly. Change, although it may be beneficial for the parent, is stress laden and causes bewilderment to the child. Change affects parents, also, even if at first it appears to be expedient. Due to the dynamics of the dissolution of marriage, the child's life is in a state of division, a tearing apart.

Divorce in itself is a highly emotional state. To let go of a spouse, to actually separate, is a painful time. Children don't have sophisticated or mature coping mechanisms. They feel abandoned and do not know how to express their loss or pain.

Many children are quick to verbalize the immediate, "Who am I going to live with?" An equally vital question for the divorcing parents: How can we handle the issue of custody in the *best* interest of the children and cause them the least amount of pain and disruption?

Divorce is a time for restructuring. Yes, it is difficult to bring order out of chaos when emotions are exploding. Obstacles, roadblocks, disagreements arise at every turn. As parents think their way through the questions surrounding custody and visitation, wiser choices and decisions can be made if hurt, anger and bitterness are set aside. Sadly, for some it may be impossible. There are no easy answers or simple solutions. But it is an opportunity to move ahead with the very best custody arrangements parents can provide for their children. This will make everyone's future more pleasant.

Several Options to Consider

Sole Custody Custody to one parent and visitation rights to the other.

Joint Legal Custody Cooperative parenting, sharing

decision-making and responsibilities concerning education, health care, religion and finances. Both parents are involved in major decisions that affect the child.

Joint Physical Custody In addition to joint legal custody, children will live with both parents on a time-share basis.

Frequent Access The non-custodial parent visits with the child on a weekly basis by a clearly defined schedule. At least two times per week.

Infrequent Access The non-custodial parent visits with the child on a limited basis. Perhaps once or twice each month. The parent could be in contact by letter or phone if visiting is impractical because of geography, ill health or other reasons.

Who Gets Custody?

There is an emerging awareness that fathers can be nurturing parents also. Fathers' rights groups are actively advocating the desire and ability of men to raise, influence and guide their children. Many fathers are interested in their children's emotional and spiritual needs. Studies show children who have *frequent* and *conflict-free contact* with *both* parents tend to survive the break-up of the home more positively.

Mothers frequently assume they will have sole custody and some refuse even to discuss joint custody. Unless fathers have the extra means to spend on additional attorney fees, they usually give up by default. In the majority of cases today, the courts continue to award custody to mothers.

There is a trend toward joint custody, which indicates parents are, at least initially, willing to work out an amenable arrangement. Statistics indicate 63 percent of the mothers are working outside the home and that fathers are picking up the slack by spending more time caring for their children.

A random sampling in Los Angeles for a one-month period in 1982 showed an increase from 5 percent to 35 percent in joint custody arrangements. Today it is considered to be even higher.

In some cases, where a parent deserts the home, disappears, refuses to participate in parenting, or is mentally ill, etc., sole custody is the only solution.

Sole custody with limited and monitored visitation would also best serve a child considered at high risk in the event a parent has physically or sexually abused the child, or the parent is a chronic substance abuser, or engages in inappropriate activities in the presence of the child.

If charges have been filed against the abusive parent, and/or the court has been presented with proper showing of the documentation, limited and monitored visitation could be ordered by the court. The court could decide against any form of visitation for a designated period, if there has been a conviction.

Joint physical custody does not necessarily mean there will be equal time-sharing of the children. Fifty percent of the time with each parent does not always serve the best interest of the child, especially for school-age children. It's workable when parents live in close proximity to each other, even in the same school district. But this arrangement needs to be flexible as the child matures and develops other interests, such as participation in sports, school activities and clubs and the need to spend greater periods of time with peers.

Cooperating parents with similar life-styles make the shuffle between homes less confusing for the children. If life-styles and rules are variant, joint physical custody still could be a viable solution provided moms and dads are considerate and refrain from making degrading statements about each other in the presence of the children. If parents are constantly bickering over stale leftovers from their marriage, it is easy to visualize children traveling from one seed bed of turmoil to another. Caught in a tug-of-war between parents in conflict, children's emotions become frayed and their self-images severely damaged.

Damage to a child's self-esteem occurs even if one parent refuses to let go of their anger and continues to speak about the other parent in a derogatory way. Not being able to let go of bad feelings is a strong indicator that a parent has not dealt with the disappointment, pain and failure of the marriage. Therapy can help such a parent work through frustration and anger in a non-destructive manner.

Visitation, a Vital Issue

Let's look at a global situation. Joe wants joint physical custody of the children. Brenda angrily refuses. She may consciously or unconsciously be trying to punish Joe. The anger she is feeling toward him is blocking her ability to think in terms of what is good for the children. For various reasons, she refuses to work out an amenable plan. Brenda wants Joe to have limited access to the children because *she* wants as little contact with him as possible.

Joe doesn't have the financial means to enter into a lengthy litigation. He becomes hostile. Having been unable to talk through their feelings to clear the air, Joe and Brenda enter the courtroom with clouded emotions and are unable to discuss the details of the custody arrangement. Both are unclear as to what *reasonable visitation* means, but anxious to finalize on their unhappy marriage, they agree to reasonable visitation.

After the papers have been drawn up, duly executed and the dust has settled, Joe then states what is reasonable in his mind. He wants to have access to his children on a frequent basis. He tells Brenda, "I want to see the children every other weekend, each Wednesday night for dinner and alternating holidays."

She replies, "Every second or third weekend is enough, and no more!" Joe now realizes, to have his children as often as he wants, he will need to return to court.

Some men have felt their manhood cut away when the children's mothers have set visitation on their own terms. Fathers can become so terribly discouraged they have dropped out of a child's life altogether! This results in a great loss for the children. In the absence of a father, children tend to indulge in fantasy, daydreaming about him, rather than knowing him and learning to deal with reality.

To complicate matters for a birth father, a stepfather may soon be involved in the rearing of his child. The father may then feel he has less worth in his role and reduces the time spent with his children. Again, each child loses by missing out on the goodness and enrichment a birth father can bring to his/her life. There is no way to measure what treasure has been lost. If our Creator didn't consider fathers to be valuable and significant, He would have made it possible for a woman to be parthenogenetic, being able to produce children without a male.

Reasonable visitation can also backfire for single moms. Dusty wanted the children to visit their father frequently. Wilson was seeing the children every other weekend, plus one or two nights each week during their separation. Dusty expected it to continue, but it didn't. She needs time-out from the children for her own well-being, and to enable her to be there emotionally for them when they are with her. Unless Dusty can communicate this to Wilson and he hears and responds, she may become depressed, hostile and less effective with her children.

Single fathers often remarry and become involved with their new spouse's children, and sometimes they start another family. With all the normal demands on the father's time, some fathers see their own children less and less.

Before the papers are drawn up, it is essential for moms and dads to state in concise terms what they need, want and what they *expect* of each other. Regular patterns of time need to be established with the non-custodial parent and the children early on. People are creatures of habit. There is a correlation—fathers who have access to their children and see them on a regular basis make child support payments.[1]

Conciliation Courts

Conciliation courts throughout America and abroad are becoming more effective in aiding parents through the divorce process and with post-divorce problems. The Conciliation Court in Los Angeles serves as a role model and has been visited by several commissions from other states and countries wishing to revise their family-law systems.

In many metropolitans, urban communities and rural areas similar conciliation courts are functioning to help separated families find peaceful ways to resolve differences. For example, Los Angeles County Superior Court has a highly successful inter-professional Family Mediation and Conciliation Service involving the bar, judiciary and behavioral sciences.

One of the objectives of the conciliation court is to provide a non-adversarial method of settling differences in custody and visitation disputes amicably. In Los Angeles County, parents are encouraged to work out their own custody arrangements in conciliation court for approval by Superior Court. Whether the plan is sole or joint, both parents are entitled to equal access to children's medical, dental, school and other records.

The good news is that even after agreements have been reached and approved by the court, should differences and disagreements arise at a later date, parents such as Joe and Brenda and Dusty and Wilson can utilize the aid of conciliation court. Using the non-adversarial method, conflicts can be resolved without expensive litigation, providing both parties will sit down and discuss the problem together.

For further assistance for divorcing or divorced parents, conciliation courts offer Divorce and Custody Seminars. Generally they are free of charge and open to anyone. These seminars help to facilitate understanding the impact of divorce on the family. Workshops cover a wide variety of divorce-related subjects, and also help the public become aware of community resources.

Child Protection Agency

Community resources can provide the help and support a custodial or non-custodial parent may need. A restructured family is subject to influences of other adults visiting or living in the home. The entrance of a stepparent may enhance, enrich a restructured family, or the opposite can occur. A stepparent may ungainfully influence the children. A non-custodial parent can feel powerless when children are exposed to questionable happenings in the home of the custodial parent. If there is evidence children are being adversely affected, or abused, the non-custodial parent can take action by contacting a Child Protection Agency in their area.

Hal and his second wife Evie have been married almost two years. They are currently engaged in such a conflict. Hal has his daughters, Abbie and Katie (ages five and two at the time of the divorce), three days and two nights each week including a split holiday arrangement, to which he has carefully adhered.

Hal shared, "After Katie saw the movie *Pinocchio* on our VCR she said to me, 'Daddy, I wish I was Pinocchio. I wish there was a wooden one of me, and a real one of me. Then I could send the wooden one to Mommie, and the real one could stay with you and Evie.'" Hal asked Katie why. She said she couldn't tell. It was a secret. Katie became depressed when it was time to return to her birth mother and stepfather.

The next week at bath time, Evie discovered large red welts on Abbie's back. Fearfully, Abbie said her stepfather had become angry with her and had hit her. Hal contacted a Child Protection Agency. After an investigation in the custodial home, the stepfather was placed on probation. Hal wondered how long his ex-wife would have continued to allow her husband to beat Abbie. Just how safe are the girls, physically and emotionally, in their mother's home?

After talking it over with Evie, Hal is seeking sole custody and is prepared to spend thousands of dollars to do so. Hal and Evie are currently being evaluated by custody counselors at the conciliation court. In the interim, the tension between the two homes is thick. Hal and his ex-wife are only able to communicate when necessary through tersely written messages. The discomfort Hal and Evie experience in returning the girls after their visits is acute. The birth mother is fighting to keep the girls in her custody. Who will win the custody battle remains to be seen.

A Case of Successful Joint Parenting

Is joint legal and/or joint physical custody, or joint parenting of any sort a viable solution? If so, then why does it work for some and not for others? Are there certain ingredients necessary for successful joint parenting?

Even after spending time in counseling, Judy and Clark could not resolve their problems. "As soon as we made the decision to terminate our marriage I moved into the guest bedroom," Judy related. "This took the pressure off. We were able to be civil with each other until we entered into a heated discussion on which one of us the children would live with. I was in the process of starting a new career, so Clark argued he would have more time to spend with the children, and was therefore better suited to be the custody parent. I became so angry I stalked out of the room slamming the door! Just the thought of not being with the kids on a daily basis was painful. I cried buckets every time I thought about it.

"After much evaluating, I had to admit Clark was an unusual father, a terrific father and would give the children the same loving, caring attention I would. His work was only five minutes from our house, and he had the same holiday schedule as the children and was able to spend more time with them. I still didn't like the idea of not being with the kids every day, but the next time we talked about custody it was a friendlier discussion. I realized we loved the children equally, and we both wanted to provide them with the least disruption. But I continued to feel guilty even after the decision had been made.

"When we told our children we were getting a divorce, the first question they asked was, 'Who is going to stay with us?' Jimmy was 10, Henry 7, and Christy 4. We told them their father would stay in the house. Then they wanted to know where I would live and if they would see me. I assured them they would. Clark and I had settled our differences.

"One day after I was settled in my apartment I said to Clark, 'I don't want to fall into the trap of being a Disneyland Mother!' Then the kids discovered they still had to pick up their clothes, unload the dishwasher, set the table and provide their own entertainment when visiting me. Just like they did at home. The constant fun only ended. They began to quarrel during the weekend. I decided on a better plan. They could come one at a time and choose a friend to bring with them. Often they chose their sister or a brother. That worked out very well. Soccer games began to fill Saturdays. Both Clark and I were on the sidelines. Sometimes Clark coached. The three kids and I have continued to attend special events, take vacations together, attend family reunions and visit Grandmother.

"I help the children with their homework two or three nights a week. I am emotionally involved with the children and they know it. I know what is going on in their lives. Clark and I make all decisions jointly and we back each other. When the kids began to play one of us against the other, we caught on real fast.

"Two years ago, our oldest son Jimmy became rebellious and extremely difficult to manage. Clark and I both went into counseling with him. We have been in crisis situations and crisis counseling with him since. I'm glad we are both here. I know *I* couldn't handle the problems with Jimmy without Clark.

"At times I wondered if Jimmy would have been so troubled and difficult had Clark and I not divorced. Sometimes I am burdened with guilt. Sometimes I cry, especially when I think how young and tender they all were when we separated.

"We all get together for the children's birthdays. Now that they are older, they like to go out to dinner. They have said to me on many occasions, 'I wish we were a family again. I wish you were going home with us. I wish Dad could go camping with us.' I say, 'This is our time together. Although Daddy and I had personal differences we have resolved our roles for joint parenting.' I try to assure them both Clark and I love them.

"The kids are well aware we have an unusual situation. Their peers who have divorced parents often say, 'Your folks sure don't act like ours! They are friends! They talk to each other! Are you sure they're divorced?'

"Someday if either of us should remarry, there will obviously be adjustments for all of us! I have given thought to my children calling another woman, Mom. Right now there isn't a significant person in either of our lives. We've lived with joint legal custody for six years, and we are committed to this until the kids are on their own!"

Clark and Judy demonstrate effective joint parenting. Their divorce was not an impetuous act. It was thought through carefully. Since they both arrived at a place whereby they could handle their emotions in a mature adult manner, they were able to work together as parents during their separation and post divorce.

Raising children is not an easy task, married or divorced. Clark and Judy's common goal to continue being on-track parents for their children attributes greatly to their success.

The Key to Success

Whether the custody arrangement is sole or joint, the key for success is dealing with and working through two separate issues.

One is closing on the marriage. It is difficult, nearly impossible, to work together effectively and harmoniously on arrangements and visitation schedules if the spirit of anger or greed has overtaken one or both parties. It is comparable to being consumed with an abusive substance that impairs the ability to think logically or act rationally and behave in a civil and polite manner.

We encourage those we counsel: Try to express your feelings. Attempt to rid yourself of anger. Say what you have to say. Clear the air. Throw away the verbal swords. If you can't do this, seek the help of a counselor who specializes in marriage closures.

If both parties are diligent at seeking emotional peace, it will be much easier to work through the second issue effectively, which is the on-going, ever-present posture of parenting the children from the broken home.

Parents who are able to encircle their children with harmony and love in their restructured families, and who can join forces with each other in facing the problems of rearing the children of divorce, will greatly aid their children in overcoming the adverse effects of the break-up of the original home.

Working Through the Issues

The following is an eight-point plan for separating parents to start the process of working through the issue of custody, visitation and handling post-divorce parenting.

One. Work out a way to talk to each other about the issue of custody. Meet in a public place if necessary. Have a neutral third party present. Use the non-adversarial method. Do your best to leave the past behind.

Two. Discuss the needs of the children. Stay with the facts. Try to use *I* messages instead of *you did* messages, or put-down phrases. Separate feelings of hurt and anger toward each other to prevent them from coloring concerns about the children. If it is impossible, get professional help.

Three. Look at some of the successes you have enjoyed in your roles as parents. Think of yourselves only in the roles of *parents* when you meet.

Four. Begin to work on a custody arrangement that is flexible and considerate of the children, and at the same time doesn't negate each of your needs.

Five. Discuss the division of time. How much time will the children spend with each parent? Is it fair to the child? Consider age-appropriate activities, socializing with peers, school work. Will you both be present for special events, if possible?

Six. In regard to visitation, talk about your expectations. Share what you want from each other. Where are the strengths and what are the weak areas in managing the children for the custodial parent? How can the non-custodial parent best help? Which one of you is better suited to meet disciplinary or other problems? How can you assist each other in your roles?

Seven. Communicate your expectations for the children. What do you hope for from them? Are you being realistic? Do you realize regardless of the age of the children, they will adjust quicker with less anxiety if both parents spend time with them that is free of hostility and conflict?

Eight. Agree to end the discussion before either of you become uncomfortable. Don't be hard on yourselves. Agree to meet again.

And remember, you have begun an important process. A good plan takes time to develop.

Note:
1. To obtain a handbook on child support enforcement, write *Child Support Handbook,* Consumer Information Center, Pueblo, CO 81004.

10

"Don't Let Anyone in till I Get Home!"

The advice of a wise man refreshes
like water from a mountain spring.
Those accepting it become aware
of the pitfalls on ahead.
—Proverbs 13:14, TLB

I MADE MANY MISTAKES," Katherine sighed, pushing her blonde hair back from her forehead. "Rodger and Betty Jean were in grade school when my husband and I got a divorce. I had custody, he had reasonable visitation rights, but I had no idea the divorce would affect them as it did. We seldom were together as a family. When we were, he and I fought a lot. I really believed the quality of our lives, the children's and mine, would greatly improve after the divorce.

"I began teaching at a nearby high school and my children were attending an elementary school only two blocks from where we lived. I thought I had it made. At that time supervised after-school playground activities were provided. My children had keys to our house, but I had instructed them to stay at school until 4:30. That's when I usually got home.

"I thought it was a great arrangement until one afternoon! Feeling sick I came home early, about three o'clock. My son Rodger was in the house with a neighbor boy, also a latchkey child from a divorced family and often left home unattended. I was shocked! Then my anger flared. I yelled at my son, demanding to know why he was home early, and what they had been doing! A strange look came over the neighbor boy's face and he left in a hurry. I could sense they had been into mischief.

"On my bedroom floor I spotted a sleeping pill and quickly checked the bottle in the bathroom. I had just refilled the prescription and nine of the fifteen were missing! Confronting Rodger, I learned his friend was into popping pills and taking drugs. He had swallowed the sleeping pills. Fortunately, the boy's mother was home and we got her son to the emergency room in time."

New Rules

That experience terrified Katherine. As a result she established a new rule for whenever she wasn't home.

"I told my kids, 'Don't let anyone in the house till I get home. Even in the evenings when there's a baby-sitter!' However, I didn't realize the sitters I hired were too young and had little if any control over my kids. One night when I returned from a meeting at school the sitter was frantic! The father of a neighbor boy was demanding to see me right away. He was threatening to call the police! His boy had tried to enter our house. My son, thinking he was now the man of the house (although I never told him he was), got his BB gun and told the boy to get off our porch. Rodger claimed he hadn't aimed the gun at the boy, but his hands had started shaking, the gun went off and a BB hit the boy's shoulder. I faced a very angry neighbor! I felt terrible. I just couldn't believe these things were happening to me!

"Often during the next year I would come home before 4:30, and my children were already playing in the house with kids from the neighborhood. If I had suffered through a bad day I blew up, and other times I just let it go. Being consistent was a real problem for me.

"Then one hot afternoon shortly after school started in September, I came home early. I discovered the entire neighborhood gang sprawled in my living room smoking pot, including my kids! I was furious and chased them all out! Then I collapsed on my bed, crying."

At that point, Katherine decided to hire a housekeeper rather than save money for a vacation. The housekeeper was stern and ran a tight ship and it didn't take her long to gain control of the situation. However, Katherine's children constantly complained that the housekeeper watched them like a hawk, and that they never got to do what they wanted to do.

When Rodger was in the eighth grade, he was able to convince Katherine he was old enough to watch his sister, and they could save money for a vacation. "A horrible mistake," Katherine said sadly. "By then both of my children were in junior high and were pot users. Whenever I tried to talk to the children's dad about the problems I was having, he would tell me what a terrible mother I was and that the divorce was all my fault. Obviously, he wasn't any help to me. I didn't need to hear any of that!"

Grown-up but Hurting

School days are over for Katherine's children. They are in their early 20s now. Recently Rodger broke up with the girl whom he had been living with and really cared for because they were constantly fighting. Afterwards he felt deserted and was suicidal. At this conjuncture he shared with Katherine for the first time the parallel feelings of devastation and desertion he experienced when his dad left at the time of the divorce.

Betty Jean along with using drugs had serious emotional problems. But when she turned 20 she began to find her way out with the aid of therapy. She discovered further help by turning her life over to Christ and by actively participating in a Christian support group. Betty Jean is expressing her feelings to her mother. Both of them, learning to let go of their defenses, are working through issues of the past. They are well on their way to healing their relationship.

Looking back, Katherine realizes she never should have *assumed* her children would do as they were told. Even before the divorce, she evaded being consistent in setting limits and following through with discipline when the limits were tested. She often felt she was not in control. In fact, her children thought discipline was a joke.

Before the divorce when the children were naughty, their dad would take them down the hall to their bedrooms saying, "You kids aren't being bad, you are good kids. Your mother is the one who thinks you are being bad." In the bedroom the father spanked pillows, while the children faked cries of pain. The three of them thought this was a wonderful joke on Mom. And it grew into a great secret they kept for years.

Since the children had grown up with conflicting ideas about what kind of behavior was acceptable, Katherine's job as a single parent became even more complex! Their father's joke set into motion that it was OK to fool Mom, that it was OK to do thing behind her back.

Katherine's story is sad. However, there is much we can learn from her experiences. Katherine hopes other parents and latchkey children will benefit from her mistakes. This is why she is willing to share her story.

Supervision Is Vital

Children living with one parent need adult supervision even more than children who live with both. Latchkey children can't be expected to be responsible for themselves. They have been hurt by the break-up of the family structure, and have been traumatized by the dynamics of divorce. They need, even crave, nurturing, direction and limit-setting from adults. To assume children will do as they are told is not a valid assumption. Children left to their own devices grow wildly like weeds in a garden left unattended. It is fair and reasonable to openly discuss family rules and limits, and what disciplinary measures will occur if they choose to disobey. After an agreement has been reached, ask the children for feedback so you know they understand and there has been clear communication.

There are no easy answers, but there are various avenues to be explored to locate adequate supervision. Not everyone can afford a housekeeper, but there may be someone in the neighborhood who can watch the children until Mom or Dad gets home from work. Possibly a relative living in the area can help. Or a relation living in another community or state might welcome the chance to live in another area. In exchange for a place to live, they could help take care of the children. Divorce forces one to be creative!

Talking with other latchkey parents can be informative and helpful. Perhaps you can work out a collective arrangement. Peggy, a single mom, returned home from work one winter evening and found her daughter trembling in the cold on the front porch. Her daughter's hands were like ice. She had lost her key and couldn't get into the house. Peggy has now contacted two neighbors who are glad to help out. She has placed extra keys with both, using one neighbor as a back up in case the other isn't home. Checking with social services in your area may surprise you. In many communities there are after school programs and childcare centers, as well as other available services.

Latchkey children need structured supervision. Leaving them in a park or library, unless there are specific programs with adequate personnel to supervise, could be dangerous. There are many pervasive, sick and demonic elements in our society that are beyond our control.

Check It Out!

Check your home for prescription drugs, patent medicines and pills of any sort. Place them out of reach of small children. Unless you can lock up guns and have complete control of access, remove them, as well as hunting knives, or any dangerous weapon. Talk to other latchkey parents where your children play to be sure their houses are safe. There are grim statistics concerning the accidental and otherwise use of all the aforementioned items in the home.

Don't assume all baby-sitters will fulfill your requirements until you have checked them out. Be alert for any unusual behavior. Don't tolerate secrets sitters might have with your children. Teach your children to know the difference between good secrets and bad secrets. Let them know if there is anything they are uncomfortable about, they need to talk it over with you. Unfortunately some baby-sitters have been known to be abusive physically, mentally and/or sexually. These offenders may be pleasant, mild-mannered, acquiescing and display a positive interest in their charges. On the surface they may not appear to be questionable. This is another reason why it's important to have good, healthy, open communication with your children.

In Case of Emergency

Would your latchkey child know what to do in an emergency such as a fire, a sudden violent storm or a major earthquake? What if your child came home and discovered a broken window or the front door standing ajar with the possibility that an intruder was burglarizing the interior of the house? In all probability there will be occasions when the children will be home alone. Gently talking over the *what if* situations ahead of time could make a tremendous amount of difference, should a disaster occur. Children who are aware are safe children, and will feel more secure and comfortable since their parent took the time to talk to them in a caring non-threatening manner.

Supervision, protection, a safe place to live, consistent and fair discipline, food, clothing and education are necessary for any child. In addition children need emotional support. A child from a broken home living with one parent has even more emotional needs. Divorce creates a multitude of change. The way in which children of divorce, exclusive of age, learn to handle the multitude of variables created by divorce greatly influences what their reactions will be, and how they will cope with life when they are older.

For many children, divorce is like a meteorite suddenly crashing into their prize glass fishbowl. The injured fish lies gasping, dying on the floor. The thick glass walls lie shattered, water running in all directions. The child looks on feeling helpless, desperately wishing there was something he could do to make it all better, make it like it was before. But deep inside, the child fears it will never be the same again.

Like the broken fishbowl, divorce shatters the family

structure and everything seems to be in a state of chaos. The child is instantly fearful but may not show it. Fear may be masked with anger or ambivalence. This is why it is necessary to have defined limits as well as consistent discipline administered firmly but gently. Limit-setting and follow-through provide the *structure* he or she needs to be able to make adjustments to the restructured family unit.

Loving Care

But, of course, the child needs more than discipline. *Care. Love. Understanding. Encouragement. Compassion.* Sitting down and talking with your child in a non-threatening atmosphere provides the needed emotional support. Then, he or she learns, based on day by day, week by week, month by month experiences, that they are important, special and cared for. As they become aware of what to expect, they will begin to feel safe and loved.

Fear doesn't disappear overnight. However, with *help, guidance* and *time,* children will eventually realize change isn't as terrifying as they first thought it would be. Good role modeling helps them to develop trust, to be hopeful and to have a less fearful approach to the unknown.

Latchkey children can develop the emotional tools they need to face the changes that will occur in their tomorrows, but in order for this to occur, they desperately need a parent or someone *trustworthy* in their close sphere of activity. They need to express their guilt, their anger and their resentments without fear. Children need a significant person, ideally both parents, who will listen to them without making judgments, and who will not be defensive or threatening. Children of divorce require extra nurturing, and, at the minimum, one parent who will look for ways to affirm and praise them frequently.

The most important task for single parents is to encourage their children to be honest in sharing their feelings, and to make every effort not to put them down for expressing themselves. This opens the channels for them to have emotional health and a sense of well-being. You may have provided a safe environment (certainly, safety is important), but if you don't know what your children are feeling, or thinking, you are leaving yourself and them wide open to harmful influences. When your children can come to you with confidence to share openly about their hopes and dreams as well as their uncomfortable emotions, you are providing them with an emotionally safe environment.

11

"My Boyfriend Did What?"

Woe unto the world because of offences!
for it must needs be that offences come;
but woe to that man by whom
the offence cometh!
—*Matthew 18:7,* KJV

IT ALL STARTED very innocently. Maggie, 37, was an attractive, lonely and depressed divorcée. After 14 years of being married to an impatient, critical alcoholic she was determined never to become involved with another alcoholic. But she was unaware of her own vulnerability. Her self-image was impaired and dangerously low. In her own words, "I was Russell's wife. I was the children's mother. I wasn't a person!"

Soon after joining an oil painting class, Maggie became friends with a woman in class. Maggie shared how lonely she felt. "But you're a dynamic, intelligent woman," her friend exclaimed. "And I know just the man I'd like you to meet!" The following week her friend arranged an informal party with a few people in her apartment.

Todd was gentle and kind. Maggie liked him from the start. Todd was an interesting conversationalist and stayed close to her. He was obviously attracted.

Their relationship clicked. "It was exciting. Sometimes Todd would surprise me by coming over before work and taking me out to breakfast. He was so polite and considerate of my needs. He listened to me intently. He was patient, very patient. He encouraged me to take more classes in the evenings toward my advanced degree, something I had wanted to do for a long time. He even offered to watch my kids if I couldn't find a sitter.

"Jason, my youngest son who was six at that time, needed more individual attention than my two other children. Often I would sit in the overstuffed rocker upstairs holding Jason on my lap and read him a bedtime story. If Todd and I were going out for a late dinner, Todd would wait for me downstairs, reading or watching TV. He never rushed me when I spent time with my kids, or anytime, for that matter.

"When my kids' hamster had a litter and one of the babies had been pushed out of the cage, Todd took the tiny animal to the veterinarian to see if the vet could save it. Another time during a rainstorm my children's dog was hit by a car. Todd crawled under the house and after rescuing the bleeding and terrified dog, he took it to the veterinarian and paid for the emergency bill.

Uneasy Feelings

"In spite of Todd's acts of kindness there was a feeling inside of me, signaling something wasn't right. I didn't understand my hesitation. The slight warnings didn't register. I wasn't into feelings then, and I pushed them down as soon as they came up."

Maggie recounted a time when her daughter Laney, 12 years old, was horsing around in the kitchen with Todd. "They were just scuffling and I thought they were having fun. She put a piece of ice down his back, and then he put an ice cube down her front and *held it there.* I thought that was a strange thing to do, and said something to him about it. He shrugged it off. On another occasion I was sitting on the patio, and she and he were wrestling on the lawn. She was lying face down and he was sitting on her, tickling her. I yelled, 'Get off her!' I felt uneasy about what was going on.

"At one point I looked at Todd and thought to myself, this man has me hypnotized. Why does he have this strange effect on me? I wanted to say to him, 'Get out of my life.' But I didn't, because I discounted my feelings and rationalized, he's a good friend; he's kind and encouraging. Something must be wrong with *me!*"

About that same time, Todd, out of the blue, openly shared with Maggie a sexual fantasy. The fantasy seemed weird, offbeat, and it disturbed her. Again she felt she should break off their relationship. Maggie talked this over with a friend. Her friend urged Maggie to pay attention to those uncomfortable feelings, and she also encouraged Maggie to end the relationship. After a tremendous struggle with herself, Maggie finally told Todd she didn't want to see him any more. He was extremely upset, and apologized for telling her his fantasy. But after a few weeks he moved to another state for business reasons.

"The children's father continued to criticize me, and took his anger out on the kids. Frequently, when he had the kids for the weekend he drank too much. My children had frightening experiences and several brushes with death on the freeway when he was drunk!

"I joined Al-Anon, because Al-Anon is for relatives of alcoholics. I tried to learn to be good to myself and to love myself. But it didn't come easily. Someone in Al-Anon said, 'Put your arms around your shoulders and give yourself a big hug.' Another one said, 'Put a sign on your bathroom mirror that says, you're beautiful.' I followed their advice, but I soon took the sign down. Somehow it reminded me of Todd. I missed him. I missed our friendship. I missed his encouragement."

A Troubled Teenager

"There had been no one in my life who had filled Todd's place. So when he returned to the area two years later and wanted to see me, I was in ecstasy! We picked up our friendship as though he had never left. We went to plays, museums and did interesting fun things.

"Laney, almost 16, was panic-stricken. In my state of happiness her distress didn't register in my mind. But I began to be puzzled about her behavior. She was seldom at home, spending most of her time at a girlfriend's house. If she was home, and Todd hugged me, like a small child she would try to come between and separate us. I asked myself why, but then quickly pushed the question out of my mind.

"One night Laney was waiting for me, sitting on my bed brushing her long hair. I could see she had been crying. With words coming with great effort, she revealed Todd had been bribing her to go to bed with him, offering her money and the use of his car. He even wanted to buy her drugs. She was angry and told him she didn't want any of his *favors!*

"Todd? Gentle, kind, considerate Todd? He wasn't the type to do something like that! I didn't believe her. I couldn't believe her! *It's not true,* I thought. *She's fantasizing. This is another wedge she is trying to drive between us. Before Todd returned she and I were going shopping and out to dinner. She's angry and jealous Todd's back taking my time.* Then I heard Laney's voice breaking through my thoughts. 'Todd uses drugs!' I couldn't believe that either! It was unreal! Todd—drugs? I refused to believe her.

"But the next day I confronted Todd with what Laney had said, and of course, he vehemently denied it. What did I expect? Todd became very angry. He claimed he was being falsely accused; his reputation was at stake! He said it would be wrong to let Laney get away with those lies. He demanded she'd be punished.

"That evening I told Laney Todd had denied everything. She became defiant. I couldn't manage her. As soon as the school semester ended she went to live with her favorite aunt and cousins. At first, I was glad she was gone.

"Then one night Laney called, long-distance. There was unmistakable fear in her voice. She said she met someone who reminded her of Todd, and that there still were events she hadn't told me. At that moment for some reason I began to believe her. I'm embarrassed I still tried to push my feelings down. Believing my daughter came slowly, but it came. *Thank God!*"

Before the summer was over, Todd was gone, the relationship ended. Even so, Laney wouldn't talk to Maggie. Eventually, Maggie's oldest son Greg started the dialogue. Todd had been after him too. Greg claimed he could run faster and was able to get away. Greg knew what was going on, but he was afraid to speak up. He also was confused because Todd treated his mother so well.

With a tremendous amount of pain, Laney finally told her mother about the molestation. Little by little the truth unfolded. At first it was fun being with Todd. He developed a relationship with Laney and her brothers playing ball. Then tag. Later it became a cat and mouse game. Todd would catch Laney and let her go. This went on for months. Laney enjoyed Todd's playfulness. He was so unlike her father.

Then one afternoon Todd caught Laney and held on to her. He tried to kiss her and touch her in inappropriate places. He told her he wouldn't hurt her, and threatened her if she told her mother. Maggie wouldn't believe her, he said. It was all her fault anyway, he charged. Laney felt dirty, confused, angry and ashamed.

Laney lived in a state of high anxiety. She tried to anticipate when Todd would be visiting and would escape to a friend's house, or hide upstairs.

Seven years later, at age 23, Laney is still struggling with trust. She has tried to develop a relationship with her father, which hasn't been easy. It's still hard for Laney to process all that has happened to her and to be able to sort out her feelings. She hasn't recovered from the effects of the molestation and has great difficulty relating to men as well as trusting them. Laney sees her therapist from time to time attempting to work her way through the rage that still boils to the surface.

The details of the molestation were excruciatingly painful for Maggie to hear. "I was blind. I allowed it to happen. I will never get over it. If I saw Todd today, I don't know what I'd do, but I know what I'd like to do! *Kill him!*"

Living with Painful Memories

How do you live with the pain and the bitter memory? Maggie has asked herself that question many times. Today with the aid of therapy, self-introspection and a close scrutiny of her past, Maggie has a clearer understanding of how her own childhood affected her.

She received little in the way of nurturing from her church-going parents. She can remember being picked up by her mother, a busy farmer's wife, and being carried on her mother's shoulder. But there is no memory of warmth. Maggie is still waiting for her mother to tell her she is attractive. Anything positive will do.

There are only two times Maggie can remember feeling connected with her father and comfortable in his presence. "Once when I was a young girl, sitting on a stairwell feeling sad and depressed, which I often felt, my father sat down next to me, looked me in the eye and said, 'I know how you're feeling.' The other time occurred at age 14 when I started to smoke. I knew one of my sisters would tell our parents, so I did. My mother was angry, but my father, much to my surprise said, 'I understand how kids are.' When mother left the room he offered me a drag from his cigarette."

At age 18 Maggie left home and paid her way through college. "When I returned home for a visit during spring break, Mother informed me she was convinced she and Daddy would go to heaven and that I wouldn't. I wondered how she knew I had all those mixed up feelings about sex! I felt that was reason enough to be sent to hell. So I became an atheist.

"Years later in Al-Anon I told a member, 'I can't have a higher power.' He asked why not, and I answered, 'Because he's going to punish me!' The man then quipped, 'Get yourself another God!' I answered, 'I can't do that, there's only one!' Up till then, I'd been telling everyone I was an atheist! I was sadly mixed up. The idea of believing in a loving, helpful, merciful Father in heaven was difficult and slow in coming. I suspect it was because my earthly parents were anything but!

"I know God now. I don't always feel contact with Him, but I know He doesn't move away from me when I can't reach Him! I need spiritual guidance. And I need to have the past forgiven."

Maggie fully accepts responsibility for what happened to Laney. Further she now understands how her poor self-image, insatiable craving for attention and acceptance created the vulnerable person she became. In Maggie's relationship with Todd she was receiving the encouragement, caring and nurturing she never had in childhood and ignored the clear signals that something was wrong within the make-up of Todd.

Maggie has a valuable suggestion for single parents who may be swiftly moving into such a painful situation.

"Listen to your gut level feelings; don't suppress them! If I had listened to my feelings, Laney would never have been molested. Then get help from a counselor to sort out all your needs and feelings."

There is no benefit in beating or hating ourselves for having made wrong decisions that have caused pain for ourselves and others. When pain is faced head on, it can become less hard to bear. The worst mistake we can make is to bury painful experiences and/or give up on ourselves. It's never too late to openly acknowledge hurt, self-defeating pride, guilt or anger by bringing them into light and asking God for forgiveness. This act is cleansing and therapeutic and can lead to an inner healing of our emotional being.

Nor is it ever too late to forgive, accept and love ourselves. Our Living Father never gives up on us. He is always ready to help. Help comes through His Word, His Spirit and through other people. We can work on becoming the persons we were created to be.

Maggie's story, although grievous to re-live, was told with the hopes that others will save themselves from similar pain and torment.

We need to evaluate our own self-images, our own vulnerabilities and our own needs for attention and acceptance, before we can see clearly to evaluate those of our children and loved ones.

12

Protecting Your Child from Sexual Abuse

---

*But whoso shall offend one of these little
ones which believe in me, it were better for
him that a millstone were hanged about his
neck, and that he were drowned in the
depth of the sea.*
—*Matthew 18:6,* KJV

No ONE LIKES to hear about sexual abuse of children. The subject causes great discomfort and anxiety. Furthermore, many people have difficulty comprehending why anyone would sexually abuse a child.

For centuries the subject was considered forbidden and unspeakable. But today the media has trumpeted and exploited this once taboo subject. As a result many blame the media for the apparent increase in child sexual abuse cases.

However, women in their 70s and 80s are coming forth, disclosing for the first time their experiences of childhood sexual molestation. These carefully guarded secrets and the devastating emotional traumas they suppressed for decades have finally come to light. But the jury is still out trying to determine if, in fact, for centuries large numbers of women have been sexually abused and the public is only now becoming aware of an extremely pervasive and serious problem.

One random sampling of the female population has shown that up to 40 percent have been sexually abused. A poll in Los Angeles in 1985 revealed that one in three girls and one in five boys have been sexually abused. Research indicates that about 80 percent of the molested children *knew* the perpetrator.

Perpetrators

Who are they? Often the perpetrators are close relatives such as fathers, grandfathers, uncles and cousins. Considered in most countries as crimes, these acts are known as incest. Blood-related women have also been known to sexually molest children; however, female perpetrators are far less common than males. The term *intrafamilial* is used when the perpetrators are not blood related, such as stepparents, live-in boyfriends or caretakers. Molesters can also be friends of the family, babysitters, neighbors, day-care or school personnel and strangers. Strangers account for approximately 20 percent of the molestations.

Regardless of the relationship to the child, whether the molester is a parent, grandparent, stepparent, live-in boyfriend, etc., *it is against the law for anyone to engage children in any type of sexual act. It must be reported either to the police or to a child protection agency.* Reporting is necessary for the protection of the child, hopefully putting an end to the abuse. It is also for the protection of *other* children, since probably most molesters victimize more than one child.

Child molesters are found within the range of all personality types, from all walks of life, as well as all occupations and professions. They may be gentle, kind, charming and appear to be trustworthy. However, perpetrators can also be sullen, quiet and withdrawn. Others attempt to be outrageously funny, playing the role of the clown, the entertainer or the game-player.

Perpetrators may very well be single, or they can pose as single, eligible bachelors. Their target is a single mother with young children, and they seem to have an uncanny sense for locating lonely, needy women. A lonely single mother recalled a telephone conversation she had with a smooth talking stranger one evening. When the man said, "I understand you have an eight-year-old daughter," she hung up and didn't think anything more about it. Today she is convinced he is the same man who later molested her daughter after they developed a relationship.

Sadly, those who molest others were often themselves victims of childhood sexual abuse. It is also distressing to note that women who were sexually violated in their childhood often marry an abuser, who in turn sexually abuses their children!

A molester is often unable to handle the reality of adult relationships, the tests and trials of living. With significant stress factors in the home, perpetrators look to small children for comfort. Statistics tell us children living with stepfathers can be at high risk. A stepfather living with a stepdaughter budding with adolescence might not know how to handle his confusing feelings of affection. Children are innocent, harmless, loving, trusting, not threatening or opposing as adults can be. Thus begins the exploitation which if not discovered and reported, can continue until the victim is in his/her teens, or until the child is emotionally strong enough to stop the abuser.

Often the abuse occurs over a period of time with a slow build-up of sexualized behavior. And even after the abuse has ceased, the child continues to suffer emotionally from the effects, and needs help. There are clinics, agencies and programs that specialize in treating the sexually abused child. Frequently after the abuse has been reported, and the child and his/her mother are in a program, a therapist or a social worker discovers other children in the family have also been sexually abused and need treatment. Many of these clinics and agencies are low in cost and will adjust their fees using a sliding scale according to income. The specialized help and services offered are invaluable to every member of the family.

Help for Victims

All major communities offer help for victims of sexual abuse. Look in your telephone book under *Crisis Intervention Services,* or contact the Department of Social Services in your area.

There are also clinics and programs specializing in treating perpetrators. They can be helped. Particularly the ones who have admitted to the molestation and are empathic to the child, recognizing and understanding the trauma they have caused. However, in order for the treatment to be successful, the molester must have a desire to be rehabilitated.

Sexual abuse is not a myth. Fortunately there is help after the abuse occurs. But the most important task ahead is to protect children from being molested. Single parents can help to minimize the chance of abuse ever occurring by beginning early in the life of a child with an awareness program. This program will draw a parent and a child close together as they both learn to communicate freely with each other.

Helping Children Become Aware

Begin by teaching toddlers, girls and boys, about their bodies. Not just their eyes and fingers and toes, but also their private parts using the correct terms, i.e., penis and vagina. If you have any degree of discomfort or embarrassment in communicating freely using the vocabulary for private, intimate parts, you'll need to discover why you feel uncomfortable. Talk this over with someone you respect, a friend or an educator, then proceed as soon as you are comfortable. Teach the young child *no one* except the doctor can touch their private parts. Assure them you will be there when this occurs.

Let children know they are in charge of their bodies. Teach the child it's OK to say *no!* to any touch that doesn't feel right to them. For example, if someone holds them too tight or kisses them and they feel uncomfortable, teach them they can say *no!* Practice saying *no* with toddlers and even older children, 4, 5, 6 and 7 years of age.

Talk to them about good and bad touches. A good touch is a hug, a kiss, a pat in an appropriate place given by a parent or another significant person in their lives. A bad touch is not restricted to private parts, but could also be a slap, a pinch, a bite, a slurpie kiss, etc., on another part of the body. The more open you can be with children, the more helpful it is for them.

Follow up by teaching children they have the right to set limits. When they understand this concept they will be less apt to be abused. Perhaps you might decide it's better not to encourage your child to kiss friends and relatives on the lips when the child does not want to. What are good touches and bad touches is something each parent needs to talk over and decide.

Recognize children have emotional needs. They have a need for closeness. But when children cling excessively and are overly attached, or at the other extreme are withdrawn and do not appear to want to be close to their parents, this is an indicator that there are other emotional problems that need to be checked into.

Help your child develop a healthy self-esteem. Each child is a unique creation. By telling a child he or she is special and is important, self-worth is enforced. As children grow older they require more freedom and will push against boundaries. This is normal and acceptable behavior. Allow them to make mistakes. Be an approachable parent. At each level of independence it's time to talk about new rules, new limits. As you demonstrate confidence in their ability to meet new challenges you are helping them to develop healthy self-esteem.

Programs in the Community

There are programs for prevention of sexual abuse in the community. Clara, a single parent, attended a meeting at her church sponsored by a mental health agency. She listened to the speaker discuss good touches and bad touches. Suddenly, an incident she had blocked out from her childhood flashed across her mind. She was five and a half and her family had moved into a new neighborhood. It was Easter Sunday. They were invited to a neighbor's house.

In the yard, the neighbor suddenly put his arms around Clara and breathing hard, kissed her neck and tried to hold her tightly. Clara intuitively pushed him away. In doing so, she realized she would be burned by his cigarette, but she felt that was better than the strange hugs and kisses he was giving her. As the cigarette brushed against her arm, he blurted, "Oh, don't tell your dad!"

Driving home from church Clara got the chills. She had come close to being molested and had not told her parents because they didn't have open communication. What about her children, did they feel free and open with her? Feeling a sense of urgency she resolved she needed to work on building bridges of openness and trust.

A guide for making sure your children have information about their sexuality.

1. Have I taught my children the names of the parts of their body, including their private parts?

2. Do my children know that their bodies belong to them?

3. Do my children know the difference between a good touch and a bad touch?

4. Have I taught my children the facts of sex? Do they have the information they need about it before starting school? Learning about sex in the home is far better than learning it in the street. If I am uncomfortable in this area will I seek help to become more comfortable and relaxed?

5. Have I encouraged my children to take care of their bodies? Do I, as a parent, take care of mine?

6. Do I respect my children's individuality and sexuality? Do I feel comfortable with the good feelings our bodies have? Can I talk to the children openly and freely?

A guide for assessing the emotional climate you are providing for your children

1. Am I aware of my child's need for acceptance, warmth, love, comfort, and the need to feel safe?

2. Do I encourage my children to be creative and to try new things?

3. How do I handle their mistakes? Do I realize they are children, and that adults don't do things perfectly either?

4. Do my children feel comfortable in coming to me with their failures?

5. Do I take time to sit down and discuss limits and

rules with the children, even though there are differences of opinions? Can we accomplish this without it turning into a yelling contest?

Precautions for preventing sexual abuse from happening to your children

1. Do I know where my children are? Do I know with whom they are playing?

2. Do my children understand they can say *no* to any uncomfortable touch, regardless of who might be touching them?

3. Have I encouraged my children to come to me immediately if someone they know, or a stranger, tries to lure, coax or trap them into doing anything they feel is wrong?

4. Am I aware that perpetrators can be personable and appear to be trustworthy, even showing an apparently healthy interest in children?

5. Am I aware that child molesters use food, gifts, favors, games and sometimes pornography to entice children into sexual activities?

6. Do my children know I will believe them and protect them? Could they tell me about a molestation without my falling apart? Or have I demonstrated I would be upset, and wouldn't really hear them if they did come to me for protection?

7. Do *I* pay attention to any inappropriate touch that appears to be questionable and stop it?

8. Have I done all that is reasonable to protect my children from sexual abuse? At the same time have I been careful not to instill into them undue fear or lack of trust of people?

9. Have I informed my children that help is available in the community? And that we don't need to solve all our problems by ourselves?

PART IV
Divorce and Remarriage

13

Divorce, Guilt and Remarriage

As the heaven stands high above the earth,
so his strong love stands high
over all who fear him.
Far as east is from west,
so far has he put our offences
away from us.
As a father has compassion
on his children,
so has the LORD compassion on all
who fear him.
For he knows how we were made,
he knows full well that we are dust.
—Psalm 103:11-14, NEB

BONNIE IS A SENSITIVE Christian woman in her mid-30s who desires with all her heart to live an abundant Christian life, but she feels caught in a web of her church's making, a web built for all who deviate from the "perfect Christian family." She expressed her feelings.

"I believe God may be tolerant of divorce, even allow it, but it is not His perfect will. I didn't have the usual biblical grounds like unfaithfulness or adultery. Even with those grounds I would not feel right about divorce, because I believe divorce is wrong.

"There is nothing I can do about it now. I can't go back. I feel like I am stuck as a lesser Christian. I've lost something, and there's no way to regain it. The churches of my denomination do not allow divorcées to serve in leadership positions. That is a strong message in itself. It's as if they are saying: You don't really belong; you have sinned; you have fallen from the ranks of the front-line Christians; you can be forgiven, but your record is blemished.

"Nobody says this to me, of course. But that's what I feel when I attend church. It's all very subtle, but it's there. And that's how I interpret the Bible. God can't accept me in the same way He accepts Christians who are not divorced.

"I feel so full of guilt and shame. I know I have to make the best of it and I will, but something is missing. Something is wrong in my life; something has spoiled my relationship with God."

Burdened by Guilt

Bonnie did not feel this alienation during her marriage, an unhappy liaison, a seemingly hopeless union of two mismatched believers. But after she initiated the divorce, guilt advanced upon her like crabgrass in a lawn. She became more and more aware of the enormity of her guilt and soon the wasteland of divorce became a stark reality.

Unable to throw off the feelings of guilt, those emotions spread to her children. They took on her guilt feelings and felt blame, too. They began to feel alienated from God and consequently Bonnie's children had difficulty believing in a merciful, accepting and loving Saviour. Their faith was severely shaken.

Bonnie believed deeply in marriage. She had married a Christian man and they attended church together. But during the 13 years of their marriage, they grew farther apart. Bonnie thought Al seemed so shallow while she wanted a deeper spiritual walk and spent lots of time at church. They were different in other ways too. Al liked to party, and spent money recklessly. Bonnie was uncomfortable in a party atmosphere. Al was content to remain at the educational level he had reached as a high school graduate; Bonnie took evening classes in art, music and psychology.

But the problem lay much deeper. Bonnie was very lonely. Al was not a companion or a friend. It seemed they shared nothing in common. Money matters became a burden. They sank deep into debt. After years of quiet suffering and communication at a near-zero level, Bonnie began divorce proceedings; then her guilt began.

Bonnie knew enough of the Bible to have heard the words of Jesus: "Every sin and blasphemy will be forgiven men" (Matt. 12:31, *RSV*). *Every sin includes the sin of divorce.* Finally, after talking with a Christian counselor, she was able to apply the words to herself and accept God's forgiveness.

The God of Abraham, Isaac and Jacob revealed himself as a merciful God in the Old Testament. "As a father has compassion on his children, so has the LORD compassion on all who fear him . . . . Far as east is from west, so far has he put our offences away from us" (Ps. 103:12, 13, *NEB*). This God of Israel forgave Abraham for his lies, Moses for his manslaughter, David for his adultery, Peter for his overt denials and Thomas for his stubborn doubts. Surely, He forgives divorce!

But believing these Scriptures did not change the fact that Bonnie was divorced and no longer married to her Christian husband. She therefore felt inferior. David had to live with his adultery and Moses his manslaughter; she would have to live with her divorce. For her there was simply no going back into a dead marriage. But how could she go forward?

God Offers Forgiveness

By accepting forgiveness without removing the whole load of guilt, Bonnie was unable to enter fully into what God intends for his children. God offers to forgive us our sins and wants to "cleanse us from all unrighteousness" (1 John 1:9, *RSV*). Cleansing means the removal of the past and renewal for the future.

A lady spilled coffee on the rug during a counseling session. She was very upset because the rug was new. We tried to assure her it would be all right. The next time she returned, the spot was gone. She looked at it incredulously. How did that happen? she wanted to know. A man had come a few days ago, sprayed something on the spot, wiped it a few times, and the stain was gone. She was relieved when she saw the evidence!

The God who forgives us also removes the stains. Divorce is forgivable. It is not the unforgivable sin, the one sin that will remain for eternity, the one defined as the sin against the Holy Spirit (see Matt. 12:31,32), the willful and continual rejection of the witness of the Holy Spirit to the ministry of Jesus.

But the unforgivable sin has nothing to do with divorce! Therefore, the Scriptures pointing to the everlasting mercy of God and the free forgiveness of all who put their faith in Christ need to be applied to the washing away of the stain of divorce! Just as Moses was not a second-class believer because of his sin, so no divorced person should allow himself or herself to be placed in an inferior position. There are no inferiors in the Christian faith. Jesus invites us all to approach Him, and He will give us rest (see Matt. 11:28-30). At the cross of Jesus all are equally accepted. He died for all. No one is excluded or pushed to the back row!

What Is the Church's Position?

What is the position of the Church on marriage and divorce? Positions vary. Some churches are vehemently opposed to divorce. Some accept divorce on biblical grounds—unfaithfulness and desertion. These churches tend to keep the divorced in a distinct category as second-class Christians. Others accept divorce because of human weaknesses and failures, and minister to the hurting.

In His discussion with the Pharisees, Jesus talked of the conflict between the *actual* and the *ideal.* The ideal is marriage forever. Having become one flesh in marriage there is no dissolution of that bond. So it was from the beginning of the creation.

The Pharisees wanted to know why Moses allowed divorce. Jesus replied, "It was because your minds were closed" (Matt. 19:8, *NEB*). "Because of the hardness of your hearts" (*KJV*). From the beginning divorce was not the intention of God. His ideal is marriage. But in actuality, human beings are frail, weak and have fallen from the ideal. They are sinners. Sinners cannot keep the perfect law of God. They break it; they fail.

Jesus not only recognized human failure, He did something about it. He came to redeem sinners. He did not *avoid* sinners. Sinners are restored into fellowship with God through the sacrificial death of our Saviour. We are all restored into full fellowship on an equal basis.

But what if we fall again and again? What if we go astray? What if Christians divorce after accepting the salvation with which Christ has purchased us?

Restoration

The answer is that there is full restoration for Christians who divorce. If there was restoration for David, who had sung Psalm 23 and many others *before* committing adultery and participating in murder, then is there no restoration for the Christian who is divorced? To interpret the will of God, we need to consider the revelation in the ministry of Jesus Christ. What He said and did. How He behaved toward people. What He showed of God. Jesus

Himself said that His every action was determined by the Father, and was, in fact, in full harmony with the will of God. "I always do what is acceptable to him . . . what the Father does, the Son does" (John 8:29; 5:19, *NEB*).

It is vital for us to work through the interpretations of a particular church, to the revelation, teaching and truth as revealed in Jesus Christ.

Remarriage

When it comes to remarriage, the positions of churches vary widely too. Some churches refuse remarriage, even when they allow divorce on scriptural grounds. Other denominations allow remarriage only if the partner was guilty of adultery or desertion, and the one remarrying can prove innocence. Still others allow remarriage if there is repentance on the part of the person wanting to remarry. And there are a few who leave it to the individual's conscience without exerting undue pressure.

A rigid, inflexible position that preaches against remarriage has led people to choose other alternatives: living with a mistress while remaining married in name, entering a common-law arrangement, choosing to have a number of casual affairs or just living together without the legal and spiritual bonds. Are these styles of life more acceptable to the God of truth and purity? Or are our *only* choices marriage and celibacy? If that is the case, we will be wondering with the apostles: "If the relationship of the man with his wife is like *this*, it is better not to marry" (Matt. 19:10, *NASB*, italics added). What they failed to see at that time is that Jesus revealed the God of holiness and compassion, truth and grace, justice and mercy!

Divorce and the Clergy

Those who are in special service for the Lord also face divorce, guilt and remarriage. How many clergy are getting divorced? Gathering statistics is difficult. The churches are not eager to furnish information. Although the ministerial rate of divorce is lower than the national average, the effect of the model family breaking up in a parish can have dire consequences.

This is happening in all denominations and faiths. Christians who have looked up to their ministers and pastors as spiritual leaders will experience disillusionment. Children of families who have been set up as a model will ask penetrating questions. Their turmoil, confusion and guilt may be even more severe than the average youngster.

Esther couldn't handle it. She had been in the center of church life ever since she was a little girl. She knew that the people of the church looked up to her daddy and her entire family. When Mom left them and the church, Esther felt the bottom had dropped out of everything. She became moody and touchy, started picking fights with other kids, caused trouble at school and sluffed off on her homework. These symptoms revealed a deeper unrest, a loss of something significant in her life. She blamed herself. Her dream had been shattered, hers, and the Christians around her.

The congregation remained supportive of her father. He stayed as the minister of the church, but life was not the same. The support from the church, even from her friends, seemed hollow and unreal. Plastic. Her family was supposed to be perfect! Her family was supposed to live as Christians! They were to show forth Christian ideals.

How could they do that now, since Mommy had gone? Wasn't it all a farce? Hypocrisy? Mommy was not coming back home, she said. If you take the heart out, you lose everything.

Most of the people in the church blamed her mother. But she couldn't blame her, really. She blamed herself! Esther knew she had not been a good Christian all the time. She had not always been obedient. Sometimes she caused trouble, arguments. She had failed. Both of her parents had to tell her often to get to her homework, clean up her room, be ready on time, the usual things of growing up. Now everything was accentuated in her mind as the cause of the unhappiness before the family fell apart, and she felt guilty.

The people in the church didn't understand what had taken place behind the scenes in her house. They weren't there. They couldn't observe. So, how could they bring any true comfort to them now? Esther felt no one really understood what she had experienced in her Christian family, and none of her friends knew what it was like to be a minister's daughter. They couldn't help her either.

Esther began to wonder how long Daddy would be able to remain with this church. Would he be accepted anywhere else? Another congregation would not want to hire a divorced minister with children. And if Daddy remarried, then what?

Esther didn't know whether she could accept another mom either. The one person in her life who seemed close now was her dad. They had a special father-daughter relationship that developed as a result of this crisis. He seemed to understand what she was feeling. But if he married again, where would that leave Esther?

Esther did not feel close to God either. Yet she had to

pretend in church that somehow, everything—including her Christian life—was alright, in spite of her guilty feelings.

A Spiritual Crisis

For Christians, the divorcing process is a *spiritual* crisis! Healing can come through the caring community and through Christians who minister compassion in the name of Christ. Divorced people commonly feel like a burden to their friends, and need reassurance that others do care enough to include them. If Christians can and will embody the love of God as revealed in Jesus Christ, and carry the faith into every area of life, healing will take place.

We are to care for one another, encourage one another, love one another, and build ourselves up in our most holy faith (see Jude 20). This is how guilt is overcome in the Body of Christ. Jesus wants to restore the sinner, just as He brought Peter back from the brink of disaster.

And that's what happened to Bonnie, in spite of her rigid teaching of the past. She came under the influence of the gospel lived out by compassionate Christians. In time, she was able to make complete peace with God and accept herself as a divorced Christian.

Then Bonnie remarried. That step was difficult for her as well. She formerly believed she would heap sin upon sin by marrying again. But through counseling and a personal search, she began to believe in a more loving Father, revealed by our Lord Jesus Christ. She came to see Him in a new light and that made her feel free. Bonnie still struggles occasionally with vestiges of guilt, but her faith grows and her spirit is strengthened because she no longer emphasizes the commands of the law over the positive affirmations of Scripture. She leans more heavily on the redemptive grace of Jesus.

Bonnie's struggles were long and difficult. Today she is sensitive to other people who are hurting and very capably helps others because she believes fully in the forgiving love of Jesus Christ.

Divorce and remarriage are facts to be dealt with. The Scriptures hold up the ideal of marriage and present a loving, forgiving Saviour who not only talks about matters of divorce but also accepts people shattered by guilt. It is wise for us to keep in mind these questions:

- What is Jesus like?
- How did He live out the will of God?
- What characterized His life and ministry?
- Why did He clash so vehemently with the legalists of His day?
- Do we catch in His life a sympathetic understanding of people and their problems? The ministry of compassion?
- Who did Jesus turn away, and who did He invite?
- Who is the God whom Jesus reveals, accepting us into a relationship with Him now and forever?

14

Learning from an Abusive Past

*A man who refuses to admit his mistakes
can never be successful. But if he confesses
and forsakes them, he gets another chance.*
—*Proverbs 28:13,* TLB

Is VIOLENCE AN ISSUE single parents need to be concerned about? We believe it is. People are often attracted to the same personality type and in a subsequent marriage often suffer further abuse.

If you have been exposed to abuse in childhood, or were married to an abuser, or know someone who is caught in the dilemma of violence in the home this chapter is especially for you.

Nancy's suitcases were packed. She stood undaunted in the doorway with her two small children. "You'll never hit me again! Unless you agree to counseling, the kids and I are leaving now!"

For nine years of her marriage, Nancy, a beautiful church-going redhead had devoured books on how to become a fascinating woman, a good Christian and a submissive wife. But nothing worked to stop Matt, a tall, good-looking, church-going Mr. America truck driver from being abusive. "I was sick of Matt tripping me, spitting at me and hitting me! And I was tired of living in fear!

"When Matt drank his personality changed and he became hostile and belligerent. This happened at least twice, maybe three times each month. But the next morning he felt so badly after hurting me, I believed he would stop. I guess I lived in a dream world. Finally I stood up to Matt."

Advances and new fronts in women's rights, human

rights, heart transplants and star wars technology have not alleviated violence on the home front! Nancy took a brave and difficult position with her husband standing within striking distance!

Men who batter their wives were once considered only a fringe element of a seamy segment of the population. However, violence is now viewed as occurring in a significant cross section of society. Media coverage has been instrumental in opening the kitchen, the living room and bedroom doors, at least a crack.

Statistics often are conflicting and do not provide the entire picture but the immensity of the problem is a valid concern. So much so that a Task Force on Family Violence was established by the U.S. Justice Department to study spouse abuse and other forms of violence in the home environment. According to the Department of Justice, in almost three quarters of reported spouse assaults, the victim was divorced or separated at the time of the incident. This finding suggests that battering may be more prevalent than currently estimated, since most incidence surveys limit their samples to married couples. Bettering is the single major cause of injury to women, exceeding rapes, muggings and even auto accidents, according to a report by William French Smith, U.S. Attorney General, 1983.

Demographic surveys indicate men who physically injure their wives crisscross all socioeconomic levels. Education or affluence does not prevent a husband from battering his wife, nor does the lack of status or success. However, there are common factors. Lack of self-esteem for one. Moreover, men who are violent often were treated in a like manner, or witnessed abuse as children. Therefore, the abuser's children are also considered at risk! Unless intervention occurs, an on-going spiral can continue, since there is a high probability the abuser's off-spring will also become violent, hurt others, or injure themselves by living irresponsibly and recklessly.

The Abuser and the Abused

Separated women seeking aid at battered women shelters often disclose to a counselor that they grew up in a family where there was violence, or other forms of abuse such as sexual or substance abuse. Another familiar ring in the case studies of abused women is a low self-esteem, and the lack of awareness that there is a choice, instead of *putting up* with the violence. Battered women often believe something they did caused their husbands to become angry, and have even accepted blame for the abuser's violent approach to coping with interpersonal problems.

When Nancy went for counseling she received a shock. "The counselor said I also had a problem. That made me terribly angry at first! He said I had allowed the abuse to continue for too long a time before I took a definite stand. Matt blames his parents for his violent behavior. For me, well, my mom was a functioning alcoholic and divorced my dad when I was 14. There always seemed to be major problems in our home. Divorce turned my mom into a bitter woman, even more so after my dad died a few years ago. Neither Matt nor I had good role models."

Abuse Is Criminal

Battery against a marriage partner is considered a

crime and since very few abusers seek treatment voluntarily, the abused woman needs to take steps to save herself and her children. Many spouses wait too long before they separate and seek help. By then the hurts have become mountains, and the patterns of destructive living too deeply ingrained. Often divorce is then inevitable. Some suffer from paranoia. They threatened to leave once, but they didn't. If they did leave, they were brought back with even more brutal force. Now they have an unwritten rule for themselves: Don't try it again! There is nothing you can do to escape his heavy fist. He will come after you. Suffer, endure and pacify him.

Along with the suffering a battered wife is convinced she must do everything perfectly. There isn't any middle ground. Even if the abusive husband has an extramarital affair, his wife thinks: Something must be wrong with me. I am not performing well enough sexually. The house isn't clean enough. His shirts aren't white enough. Somewhere, somehow, I must be disappointing him. If everything is taken care of, he wouldn't need to have another woman on the side. He is angry. Something I am doing is driving him away. I must try harder to please him.

Danger Signals

Violence, extramarital affairs, abuse of any type are indicators of deep, difficult problems. Sometimes before marriage there are slight indicators of problems ahead— but the problems become more obvious shortly after the ceremony. Tiffany, wiser now, can look back and see the potential problems she didn't see when she was 18. Her marriage with Lonnie ended in divorce.

"We were in our senior year in high school and were

planning a big church wedding. One night after a basketball game I stood talking with my friends. When Lonnie came out of the locker room he became extremely jealous. Holding onto my arm tightly, he said I couldn't talk to them any longer. I told him, 'Friends are important to me, and if this is the way you're going to be, I don't want to marry you! I don't even want you to take me home tonight!' Looking straight into my eyes, Lonnie pleaded passionately, 'Tiffany, if you leave me, I'll die!' From that moment on I discounted my feelings and my needs. I took on the responsibility for his entire life. Everything that was wrong became my problem, and everything that went right was to his credit.

"After we were married he occasionally hit me, then gradually he became more and more abusive when he became angry. I thought it was my fault. I convinced myself I was doing something that caused him to be violent. *I even accepted total responsibility for his extramarital affairs.*

"Finally I took courage and talked to our pastor and he referred us to a therapist, but Lonnie refused to go. I had been married 14 years and we had two children before I finally learned my way of thinking was sick! After our divorce, I learned in group therapy it takes a strong person to say, 'I care for you very much, but if you kill yourself, that is your choice. It's not my problem!' I wish I had known that years sooner. But I have learned beating myself with what I *didn't* know at 18 is self-defeating and destructive. Lonnie still blames me for the failure of our marriage. *But I'm thankful I don't buy into that kind of thinking any more!*" Having spent an insightful time in therapy, Tiffany is not going to make the same mistake again, by marrying another abuser.

Early on in a marriage there can be red flags. They signal help is needed. Jamie wanted to talk to her mother, someone! anyone! about her sex life. She was desperate. "Sex with Bill was real kinky! But I was afraid Mom and my friends would think *I* was weird. So I went to the bookstore and bought books on the subject. One Christian author implied, if *both* people enjoy it, it's OK. But I didn't enjoy it! I couldn't tell Bill he was actually hurting me. Once I told him I didn't like what he was doing and he angrily claimed I was threatening his masculinity. He couldn't deal with it. When I tried again, he smacked me! If I crossed him in any matter, he beat me at night in our bedroom after the kids were asleep. I convinced myself that my mom and other women must be going through the same thing; they just didn't talk about it.

Permitting Abuse

"It wasn't until all three of our kids were in school and I started college that I discovered *I was weird* for letting this go on and on. I went to see a counselor on the campus. It was like a dam that broke. I didn't hold anything back. Bill went once and said he wouldn't go again. On the way home, he was furious because I told the counselor about our sex life and his abusive behavior. He shouted he was a good provider, and I should have no complaints! And that I was a crazy woman! He made several violent threats telling me I couldn't go back to the counselor, or college! That did it for me! I had found something good and I wasn't going to give it up. I was too scared to be near him after that.

"The next day while he was at work, I packed the kids' clothes, picked them up at school and drove nonstop until we reached my parents' house in another part of the state. For the first time I told my mom and dad what had been going on. They were shocked, but they were supportive, much more than I ever dreamed. The kids and I stayed with them for over a year. Bill and I were divorced after being married for 12 years. I wish I had sought counseling sooner. I can see living in that weird way for so many years has affected my children."

Existing in an abusive environment is not only painful for the enduring spouse, but often children are the recipients of violence as well. This can cause children misconceptions about interpersonal relationships. Many will experience difficulty in facing reality, especially if their feelings and painful memories have been suppressed. Born out of their experiences, they may even view abusive behavior as normal. Some have thought their warped families were perfect.

Life in the Dysfunctional Family

After having been in the service, Phil returned to live with his mom who had been divorced four years.

"My dad was hard on us kids physically, me and my brothers. I saw my mom get thrown across the room and she hit a glass window. I saw her get slapped a few times. I heard yelling and crying late at night. My dad has a way of domineering and making people feel real inferior.

"My brothers and I got whippings for stealing cans of pop out of the refrigerator. We couldn't touch them. We were only supposed to drink milk or water. Dad also bought sweet rolls but only for himself; we were supposed to stay out of those also. He was good at spotting things and would punish us by hitting us with his belt. Mom would tell him to stop, but he'd say, 'Don't disagree with me in front of the kids! Don't undermine my authority!' It makes me mad now. Mom had no power to protect us from him. I guess I've always known though that nobody could stop Dad from doing anything once he made up his mind.

"There was a lot of oppression at home but I didn't know it when I was growing up. I didn't know this stuff didn't happen in other families. I never talked about what went on in our house. I thought our family was pretty near perfect. We kids always behaved good when Dad and Mom were around. When I was a kid, I knew Dad wasn't exactly *perfect*, but I thought he was cool. I admired him. He was a good man. It always seemed like he had friends, but when I started looking back, I realized they didn't stick around. He always had new friends. He had a way, and a certain look. Since the divorce, he has a crazy look.

"During the last few months in the service I thought about how I let my dad down. I wanted to play soccer, but he said it wasn't physical enough. He wanted me to play football because he had played. I hated football, but I stayed in football for seven years just to please him. I had nothing positions on the second or third string, just filling space. Dad didn't like it. Then he wanted me to go into the Marines, and I went into the Army. Dad would call me and say I was letting him down and that I was a failure.

"While I was in the service I had a girlfriend who was divorced and had a child. She didn't whip her kid at all! This little boy talked back to her, and I said, "Hey, why don't you hit him?" To me, it was normal to be hit. I really thought if your kids do something wrong, you beat them. After talking with her I began to see you don't have to beat your kids. There were times when I deserved it, I know, but not for stealing a cola or a sweet roll! Just before I got out of the service I was still crying at night. Then I gave up on working for a good relationship with my dad. I had tried so long to please him. Now I know it's impossible for me to please him.

"I'm doing lots of thinking. Our whole family, except for Dad, has a tendency to pull away when we are upset. I normally go to my room and just sit on the bed. Sometimes I live in my fantasy world without problems. What I really want is for Mom to talk to me. As long as we are talking, and listening to each other, I won't be angry for long. I ask God, 'What did I do? Why can't things go right? What did I do to deserve this?'"

In an abusive environment, parental demands are generally unfair, and have little regard for the individual's preferences, or innate abilities. Therefore, adult children of divorce often have problems accepting themselves. They perceive a parental lack of acceptance that indicates to them they are unworthy. Once they recognize the limitations and the inappropriate behavior of the abusive parent, as well as their power to overcome, a stepping stone toward self-acceptance will have been laid.

Distorted Thinking

Coping with normal frustrations encountered day by day can be difficult for an adult child of divorce who has been exposed to violence within the family structure. The combination of an explosive parent and a peacemaker who submits weakly to abuse can cause distorted thought patterns to develop in children. Consequently the child's energies may be poured into self-destructive behavior.

Morgan's parents divorced while she was away at college. As far back as she can remember, her parents had violent arguments resulting in heavy blows.

"Intellectually I knew why Mom was divorcing Dad, but I still felt confused and hurt. I wrote them for extra money. I got real good at playing one parent against the other. As soon as I cashed a check, I bought a large pizza with everything on it, then sat in my car stuffing myself. Next I drove to 31 Flavors and got two half gallons of ice cream. I kept shoving it in until I was miserable and felt like I would burst. But whenever I was with my family or friends, I ate lightly. Later I learned how to purge myself, and I started doing this on a regular basis. I never gained a pound. For a while I fooled myself by thinking I could have my cake and eat it too! Now I wish I had never started. It's a stupid habit and costs so much. I want to stop, but I can't. I am so frustrated and angry. Something is controlling me! I hate myself!"

Morgan couldn't express her feelings or anger when she was growing up. On the surface it appears Morgan and others like her who have repetitive compulsive eating addictions, such as overeating, or starving, or eating and purging, are being controlled by their desires for food, or fear of becoming fat. This compulsive behavior is actually the manifestation of deeper underlying problems. Whenever Morgan is frustrated or depressed she turns to food for comfort and when she is happy, it's a reason to celebrate. Whatever the occasion, food warms her stomach and brings back good feelings of her childhood—a special dinner, a breakfast at a favorite restaurant.

Morgan is being controlled by her emotions and feelings. This repetitive, punishing behavior is similar to a woman who continually allows her husband to beat her. Neither knows how to handle frustration or anger in a constructive manner. Neither have learned how to be gentle with themselves. Both think they have to be perfect. Often both are people pleasers with poor self-images who are compelled to maintain peace at all costs.

Changes do not come easily for anyone! Pain is not bypassed. But by going through a productive process of change, with a caring therapist coupled with faith and trust in a healing, loving God, we can be liberated!

Ending Abuse

Paul writes in his chapter on marriage, "Honor Christ by submitting to each other" (Eph. 5:21, *TLB*). This does not give a spouse the right to physically injure their marriage partner into submission. Nor does it bring honor to Christ if either spouse submits or yields to violence, cruelty, bitterness or hatred. The longer violence is perpetuated, the more painfully difficult a situation will become.

Christians are not commanded to put up with abuse. We must battle against evil. Seek to bring good from evil. Then if all else fails, flee! A battered spouse doesn't bring honor to Christ by submitting to beatings. Help is needed. Keeping this heavy burden undercover doesn't provide any relief. If the abuser doesn't stop, the abusee must leave. To stay in a sick situation cannot produce health.

There is more help available today than ever before. The telephone books in all major cities have listings for crisis intervention services. Local law enforcement agencies are learning more effective methods of handling home violence. Lawmakers are becoming increasingly aware of the problem, and are writing stronger laws giving more protection to the abusee.

There are shelters for battered women. Shelters generally provide 24 hours, 7 days a week service. There are hotline services 24 hours a day providing crisis information and referrals. Shelters provide a place of safety for a woman and her children. The stay can extend from 30 to 60 days. Arrangements can be made for school-age children to continue education during their stay at the shelter. A battered woman will be given information regarding marriage and family counseling, job training programs, legal help in obtaining a restraining order, and access to other available services in the community.

By contacting county or mental health departments, local welfare or social service departments, you can receive help. You can tell your pastor the entire story, not holding back to protect the abuser. If he sends you back to the same threatening situation, find another counselor. You need to get help!

Even if children aren't being physically abused, there is danger in allowing the violence to continue. Children growing up in such an environment with role models who are abusers and abusees can learn the same patterns for expressing anger. As adults, they may express their anger by committing abusive acts that harm others, or they may unconsciously choose to punish themselves by submitting to violence. Not being able to cope with frustrations, disappointments and hurts they may elect suicide. Unless the abusee seeks aid and intervention occurs the child's future remains in jeopardy.

A survey of battered wives released by the Justice Department in August 1986 shows that battered wives prominently reduce their chances of being beaten again when they reach out for help and call the police. The Bureau of Justice Statistics' survey of the effect of reporting domestic violence found that all the married women who did not call the police after their husbands beat them,

41 percent suffered repeat attacks within six months. Only 15 percent of the wives who called authorities after an assault, however, were beaten during the next half-year. This study clearly shows an abused wife *increases her chances for safety* by calling for help!

15

"Can I Make a Better Choice?"

If you return to the Almighty,
you will be restored . . . .
Then you will delight in the Almighty . . . .

You will pray to Him,
and He will hear you . . . .
And light will shine on your ways.
—Job 22:23-28, NASB

IT'S A QUESTION the divorced begin to ask eventually: Can I make a better choice than I did the first time? Statistics indicate that of all *re*marriages more than three out of four men and women have been divorced. It may be fair to state that the majority of those divorced expect to remarry.

Many people are unhappily married. One national psychologist alleges that only 10 percent of all marriages are happy. How can he be so sure of these figures? Who knows? Perhaps he has observed many unhappy liaisons. Certainly many married people want to get out of their marriages while many singles want to get in! Singles would like to be married; hence the high statistic for second marriages.

After her separation, Harriet attended a couples group at her church. "They had a party and I went. There were 13 of us. I was number 13. It wasn't any fun at all. I felt like a fifth wheel. I'd like to meet a good Christian man, but there aren't any single men at my church."

Carl's wife left him after 20 years. "As far as I was concerned we had an enjoyable marriage. She didn't think so and refused to return. I walked into the office of a friend who is a real estate agent and I felt jealous. He had a wonderful family picture on the wall. I looked at it and felt a sense of loss. I'm disillusioned. I need a good relationship! But, can I make a better choice next time? One that will last?"

First Things First

Making it on our own is a prerequisite for marriage. Many jump hastily into a new relationship only to discover they have made a terrible mistake. They marry because they're needy and lonely. But statistics indicate more second marriages fail than succeed! That leaves many facing a third go-around.

After a divorce there must be a time to heal. There is a natural grieving period and stages of recovery, just like after an operation. Following a divorce individuals need to transcend anger and bitterness and most likely disillusionment and depression. They need not be in a hurry.

People who don't wait before they are through grieving may regret their new involvement. The grief period may take an average of six months, some say a year, some longer. Healing depends upon the individual. But those who begin to date too soon are still on the rebound, not yet in charge of their emotions.

Those who have experienced divorce need not settle for someone with whom they have little in common. They need not enter into a relationship merely to fill a void. They need more than temporary fulfillment; they need a relationship that will endure.

The question of remarriage is a serious one.

One father said, "I don't want some jerk bringing up my children." This made him stay in a difficult, uncomfortable marriage much longer than he wanted to.

A divorced mother was eager to know, "Whom can I trust to become a reliable father to my kids?"

Because children are very important to parents, it is safe to affirm that if it weren't for the children, there would be far more divorces! Even though we don't want to marry a person simply to fill the role of parent to our children, we need to make sure of the integrity and character, as well as the dedication to parenting of the person, to whom we entrust ourselves and our children.

"I can't handle dating lots of people," admitted Joyce, a timid, sweet divorcée in her late 30s. "I don't like the immature guys that are cruising out there, and I don't want somebody else's cast-off baby. Certainly not for my kids. I find that I don't have the energy or enthusiasm for dating. I tried meeting men one night at a party, but I returned home early. I hated it. These people couldn't talk to each other until they had several drinks. They were half-married and half-unmarried. I don't want to be a part of that sleazy scene."

A Time to Reflect

Happiness need not be born in a marriage and killed by a divorce. This is a time to struggle with many questions and we need to make sure of what we want from life. As we think about dating and the future, we need to set goals and determine how to reach them. Probably the foremost question to raise is not, How can I prevent marrying the same type of person again? but rather, How can I prevent being the same kind of person again?

We need to find out what we have learned about ourselves from our first marriage. What contribution did we make to the failure of our relationship? How can we change? What do we need to work on?

What about our attitudes, habit patterns, ways of relating, reactions, anxieties? Who are we? Are we free to be ourselves or do we feel tied up, unable to change?

If we were constantly nagging and critical and drove

our partner away with our sharp tongues, have we become aware of what we have done? Have we been able to change? With God's help do we believe we can change our form of behavior? Will we allow the Holy Spirit to make us more sensitive to our own shortcomings? Can God's Spirit direct us into more positive patterns for living?

If we were anxious and worried and drove our partners crazy because of money, we need to recognize what we did and find out why we were overly concerned. How can we change our anxieties about money? Money arguments are probably the major cause for many divorces.

On the other hand if we were financially irresponsible, spent money freely and ran up charge accounts, we must discover what made us do this. No one can remain happily married to someone who spends money wildly and brings the family to the brink of ruin. Even the greatest romance will be undermined by irresponsible spending.

These are just a couple of illustrations. Examine yourself. Discover what you need to work on. This is hard work, but with a sincere desire and the Lord's help you can begin to change.

Meeting People

Now, where can we meet people? Friends and family will step in to help us meet people who are eligible, but that seldom works out. Especially if we are invited to dinner by a couple who just happen to have an eligible person at the dinner table to introduce to us. This is a set-up, and we know it.

Some Christians frequent bars. They have heard this is *the* place to meet people. It may be, if you're just looking for a one night stand, but not for a lasting relationship!

What are you interested in and what do you enjoy doing? Determine these things, then join groups or clubs that center around such activities. For example, do you like to swim or bike or hike? Find groups in your community that sponsor organized activities and meet people who have common interests. And of course there are churches and single groups to attend.

As dating becomes more entangled and centers on one serious relationship, how do we discuss these matters with our children? How can we let them know what we're feeling? How do we prepare them for the future?

If the first marriage has been relegated to the past and properly closed, we are in a position to tell our children that we have needs, too. Children can relate to that. They may become receptive to the idea of a new marriage if we have been clearcut and forthright. We need to discuss our relationships and the possibilities of another marriage.

But remember, marriage is primarily for companionship and not to find another parent for our children. When the children are grown, we need to be able to enjoy living with the person we've married.

Spiritual Closure

There is also a spiritual dimension for closure, especially if we are Christian and married with the belief that our marriage was in the will of God. We may have prayed about our first marriage and asked for God's will. We felt led into that relationship. Maybe we were both believers and trusted God when we took that important step. What happened?

Many things could have gone wrong, but the nurture

and developing of the love relationship did not emerge as priority. What is the priority? Many people neglect to work at love in marriage and become preoccupied instead with making a living. A husband expects to succeed. He drives ahead in the business world. He wants to make a go of it. All for the family, of course. He convinces himself he needs to earn a good living. Slowly but surely his own successes and achievements emerge as priorities. In churches some ministers are trapped into thinking that this is *their* congregation instead of the Lord's, and ministers' wives may resent that the church is number one in their husbands' lives.

What is the top priority for marriage? Reading the Bible and going to church does not take the place of working on the basic relationship. Some Christian marriages have fallen apart in spite of church attendance and family devotions.

Now is the time to close this past marriage spiritually. Can we confess our sins or do we want to maintain our innocence? If we are willing to repent and accept the forgiveness of God, we can close this chapter of our lives. We can begin anew with more understanding, more faith, more love because we have accepted responsibility and have been willing to learn from the past. Lasting good can emerge from hard but honest self-examination.

Assuring Our Children

As we face our futures with anxiety, we need to remember our children have fears, too. They worry whether they will have a place in our lives if we should marry again. If they had a primary place before, where will they fit in when we have a new man or woman in our lives?

Will this new person take over? Will we make time for the children? How will we be able to meet their needs? Will they feel neglected? We need to be honest in meeting these needs and fears in our relationships with the children and our new spouses.

We need to talk about it and reassure them with phrases like:

- You are important to me.
- We will do things together.
- I always want to know what is happening to you. You can come to me. I will find time to be with you.
- I love you and maybe we will all love one another and become a happy family.
- I believe the Lord is guiding us into this new life. I've been praying about it and I feel peaceful.

Discuss Rights

It is essential to prepare children for the changes with honest dialogue. Discuss the rights as well as the needs of all the people involved. Some counselors even suggest drawing up a contract after all parties have mutually agreed on the terms. Children are persons who have rights. Let them know we respect them and will listen to their requests.

Let's suppose a divorced woman with two teenagers decides to marry a man whose business will necessitate a move from her area. Her children are entrenched in school and church and have all their friends in the community. A daughter in high school has only one year remaining before graduation. The other daughter is in the eighth grade. Both teenagers are dead set against leaving their friends and familiar surroundings. Their mother is very much in love and believes this is the man God chose for her, but marrying him will mean moving to another city.

An honest discussion of the problems is the best solution. We can't proceed to marry without considering the needs of everyone involved. On the other hand teenagers need not stand in the way of what we believe will be a God-blessed marriage. There are no simple solutions for complex problems. But listening to one another, taking all feelings into consideration and praying together for guidance honors everyone. When we listen in love and trust the Lord to guide us, we may come up with a creative solution—perhaps an alternative we had not previously considered. His promise is that "Light will shine on your ways" (Job 22:28, *NIV*).

A Better Choice

Harold is in his second marriage and is sure he made a better choice as both he and Carol are romantic and have much in common. "But I wasn't prepared for all the complications of a second marriage," Harold confided.

"There were many areas we didn't talk about before we married. Frankly, I didn't realize there would be so many problems. After our honeymoon I moved into Carol's house. Sometimes I feel like an intruder. Especially when Carol and her 10- and 12-year-old huddle together around the dinner table and talk about old times and look at albums. I feel it is their private party. I want to have a positive relationship with her kids, but after one year of marriage trust hasn't been built yet.

"When I discipline Carol's children it rubs her the wrong way. Carol doesn't want me telling her kids what to do. They're her kids, not mine. I really feel her kids resent my interference.

"When my 8- and 11-year-olds visit on weekends it gets tense. Sometimes I take my kids on bike rides. Then we have a good time, but I don't get the work done around the house and yard that needs to be done. I spend far more time with Carol's kids than mine. My kids resent that and Carol's kids resent my kids coming into their territory. It was different when I lived alone in an apartment. I guess that is the way it is with divorce and remarriage. I'd rather be with my own kids. I want to be there as they're growing up to have some input in their lives.

"Money matters are touchy also. I want to teach Carol's kids financial responsibility. Carol thinks I should give a larger allowance to her kids. It's hard paying child support and raising another family. Living with someone else's kids is surprisingly difficult. I wasn't prepared.

"Carol and I have to work things out. I want to give it my all. I don't want to lose all those good feelings we have for each other. We are going to have to get help because neither of us want another divorce."

Before we proceed into a new relationship we need to raise serious questions. The following are designed to aid in raising our consciousness. Perhaps after checking the list you can write out additional questions that are unique to your situation and relationships.

1. Have I come through my grieving period?
2. Have I had time to heal from my previous marriage?

3. Have I emerged from despair and depression?
4. Have I dealt with the pain, hurt and anger?
5. Is my relationship with my children moving in the right direction?
6. Have my children overcome the trauma of the divorce, and are they emotionally stable?
7. Have I resolved the issue of guilt and divorce in my own mind?
8. Do I believe I deserve:
   • to be married again?
   • to be happy?
   • to have companionship?
   • to be loved?
   • to receive God's blessing?

9. Do I want a father/mother for my children more than I want a companion for life?
10. Have I stopped blaming my former mate and examined my own faults?
11. Have I understood why my marriage failed?
12. Have I listened to the insights of a caring friend, someone in my family or a wise counselor?
13. Have I listened to my children and accepted their observations?
14. Have I changed my negative and damaging:
    • habits?
    • attitudes?
    • speech?
    • thinking?

15. Am I in touch with my feelings?
16. Have I been open and honest in my new relationship?
17. Have I shared the essentials of my past?
18. Have we discussed:
    - the future?
    - his/her children?
    - religious convictions?
    - potential problems?
    - finances? wills?
19. Have I been open and honest with my children about what is presently happening in my life?
20. Have I ignored any red flags and uncomfortable feelings in the new relationship? Am I afraid to ask my friend any questions? Can we discuss everything?
21. Have I resolved issues that have already arisen in this relationship?
22. Is my friend telling me the truth about the failure of his/her past marriage? Do I have an understanding of both sides?
23. Have I done my homework? Do I know what the truth is? I don't want any surprises after the wedding ceremony!
24. How is my new friend getting along with my children?
25. How do my children like this person?
26. Can I take on his/her children full time, part time? Have we discussed this?
27. Can I accept a limited relationship with his/her children, knowing it won't ever be like it is with my own?

28. Am I thinking of marriage because:
    - I am lonely?
    - I am already sexually involved?
    - I am so needy?
    - I want a parent for my children?
    - I am convinced this is my last chance?
    - This is the right person for me?
29. Can I see myself living with him/her when all our children are grown?
30. Do my friend and I have similar goals? hopes? dreams? life-styles? values? morals? beliefs?
31. Have I prayed about this? Have I asked God's will in this relationship?

Once the decision is made and a new marriage comes into being, children and teenagers can be supportive, especially if they have been included in the decision-making process.

16

The Anatomy of a Blended Family

By wisdom a house is built,
And by understanding it is established;
And by knowledge the rooms are filled
With all precious and pleasant riches.
—*Proverbs 24:3-4,* NASB

ALL OF A SUDDEN I had seven people to cook for! I had become accustomed to being a single mom, and I hadn't been doing that much in the cooking department. I began to work real hard but it wasn't that successful. Nine times out of ten the kids said, 'Laurie, this is yuk!' or 'Mom, this is terrible!' The whole routine. I was trying to please everybody and quickly discovered you can't, not all at the same time. But I did learn all their preferences. Then I made sure that one special main dish or a favorite dessert turned up at each evening meal.

"Very shortly I discovered the food department was only the beginning of the perplexities two families blended together struggle through to live peacefully under one roof. Charlie and I have been married for almost 11 years, and with five kids between us, his three and my two, we know our problems will never cease. But we are going to make it!"

Professionals in the mental health field and stepparents agree the world's most difficult assignment is living in a blended household! To be successful and *contented* is even more so. Second marriages often fail because moms and dads were not emotionally ready nor willing to work hard at solving the discordant complexities a blended family brings about. At the onset many parents have unrealistic expectations of their children, wanting everyone to march to the drumbeat of the newly created family.

Children in blended families are often confused and

become rebellious. They liked their families the way they were! With candor, they voice a familiar and common complaint: "Our family wasn't perfect. But it was better than living with a stepmom and *her* kids, or a stepdad with *his* kids!" They want their old family to be reunited. Their foundations have been shaken. They have trouble handling changes. Married a second time, their birth dad is suddenly upbeat, cheerful and even enjoys cooking!

"But Dad never put his foot into the kitchen before except to eat, and now he thinks he's a gourmet chef? It doesn't compute!" Cassie, age 14, bitterly complained. Changes in their parents confuse kids, and often cause them to be angry. They ask, why wasn't Dad like this in our house?

Perhaps their mom had been undemonstrative. Now she suddenly responds to her new husband enthusiastically as though he's the world's greatest! Kids have difficulty accepting any kind of change in their parents. They view their stepdad very differently from their father. Certainly with less tolerance. Therefore how can *he* be so wonderful? But parents caught up in the thrill of the new relationship want the kids to make adjustments quickly and accept the stepmom or dad in the parental role.

Undermining Change

Children will attempt to thwart these new relationships and disable the newly formed family structure. It isn't that they don't want their parents to be happy; it's because they are feeling uprooted and confused about the changes over which they have no control. They have been thrust into a new environment feeling they had no choice. This is true; they really didn't have a choice.

The transition into the new family can be made smoother and more comfortable for the child. By taking time to sit down and quietly talk several times *before* the new alliance has been formed, the child can mentally and emotionally get ready for the changes. If they are told, with little warning, "Pack your clothes, we're moving!" or, "Make room in your closet, your stepsisters are moving in!" it's no wonder they rebel.

Depending on the child's temperament, self-image and how well they have handled changes in the past, the child still might feel like a misfit in the newly structured family, even if there was a period of preparation. Especially if this all comes about within a short span of time. But if children can talk to their parents about their feelings and parents have demonstrated love, receptiveness and concern, this will help children immensely in making the transition and eventually the adjustment.

Another concern is children blaming themselves for the divorce. They can be internalizing an abundance of pain and guilt. This, compounded with adjusting to a new family, stepbrothers and stepsisters, can release a potpourri of feelings and resentments.

"And her kids are calling my dad, Dad!" Zandra, 12, stated. "It's not fair! I don't like her kids, and I don't like her! I never asked for this!" Her comments echo across the land.

Often it is hard for a child *at any age* to share a parent with a step family. This may be keenly felt if the new marriage follows closely on the heels of divorce. On the other hand, the child may have made the adjustment to the divorce, and has become accustomed to spending quality and quantity time with the single parent. Either way, the child hurts.

A Blended Family Shares

Laurie, a single mom with two children, had been living in the Northwest for most of the six years following her divorce. Both of Laurie's parents married and divorced three times. Since Laurie was eight she hasn't seen her birth mother, but she has remained close to a stepmother whom she calls Mom.

As a single mom, Laurie made many well thought through decisions. She was careful not to say anything hurtful or degrading about the children's father. She could easily have become bitter about her first marriage, due to Vic's blatant unfaithfulness. With the guidance of a skillful Christian counselor, she chose a better course.

"At age 32, through friends, I met Charlie, who is four years older than I am. I could see immediately a very giving, nurturing man, kind and good, through and through. My children liked him too, but what was more important, he warmly embraced *both* of them."

Charlie had been left with two children and a baby when his ex-wife, desiring her freedom and independence, deserted the home. He gained custody and had been alone for four years. Occasionally his ex-wife dropped in to visit the children. Charlie came from a stable, content, church-going family, and his parents are still happily married.

Charlie and Laurie discovered they had much in common, and falling in love, they considered themselves soul mates. After a few months they were married. However, like a black shroud, conflict hovered and descended upon them while on their honeymoon. Alice, Charlie's hostile former wife, entered his house where all five children were staying with a baby-sitter. Creating a great furor,

Alice swooped her children away. Charlie and Laurie cut their honeymoon short and rushed home to rescue the confused and frightened children.

Charlie put his foot down. His former wife no longer could come into the house. Filled with animosity, Alice retaliated and told her children, Monica, 12, Clay, 9, and Willie, 4, that they must never call Laurie, mother. *She* was their mother.

The first year was the hardest. "We found the companion each of us had dreamed about, and we wanted to spend time together, but all five children were determined to undermine the new family. The children all felt very insecure. It was a time of crises. Bev was now 13 and Mike 9. For the past six years they had had all my attention. Suddenly they became extremely demanding, unlike they had been when we lived in our own home. Then my daughter became withdrawn.

"Charlie's daughter Monica didn't accept me or my children. She was openly resentful. She liked everything the way it *had been* and rebelled against rules of any sort. Charlie became stronger with her and set limits. She didn't like that. When Charlie wasn't home she made crummy little comments to me, whatever suited her fancy. She didn't like the church we were attending; she didn't like the way I managed the house; she found fault with just about everything.

"All the children tried to push and pull. They played the game one parent against the other. Charlie would ask me, 'Why did you let this child do that?' I hadn't, but they said I had. 'What's going on?' we asked each other. We disagreed and then began to argue heatedly! The children took sides and egged us on. When we saw what was happening we had a discussion behind closed doors. We realized if our marriage was going to survive, we needed to stand together. There were five of them and only two of us!"

The blended family with new brothers and sisters created upheaval for the children. "Each personality was unique. We were trying to mesh the children into one happy family. It wasn't working. Lack of space also contributed to the dilemma. Before we could move ahead, we had to get rid of old business. We sold both houses and bought *our house*. But more space didn't solve all the problems.

"Monica was still very needy. We went into counseling with her, but she remained strong-willed and difficult. There wasn't enough time in each day to do all that had to be done, even with Charlie's help. So instead of working full time I began to work part time. The kids were in sport activities and Scouts. Charlie became a Scoutmaster, and I enjoyed being a team mother.

"My children were rapidly bonding to Charlie. He became special to them. On the other hand, I was always seeking his children's approval. I found that no matter how hard I tried, I wasn't going to be good enough. One can never replace a mom, no matter how poorly a mother might have behaved. For a while I was trying so hard; I was never me. It took some time before I discovered I could only be myself."

The children get lost in the shuffle of activities if time isn't spent with each individual. "The teen years must be the most fragile! Charlie and I periodically spent time alone with each child, trying hard to listen, searching for their feelings. We treated them as individuals.

"Birthdays became events, unique and personalized for each child. With so many of us, it seemed like there was a celebration each month! We made holidays a time to pull the family closer, and a reason to do something out of the ordinary. All our Christmases have been special. Early in the season Charlie and I start baking fancy cookies and making Christmas candy and plum puddings. By the time Christmas arrives, our freezer groans from the extra load. We love to stay home on both Christmas Eve and Christmas Day. We just enjoy each other, forget diets, eat a lot of good food and look at home movies and slides. The children really like the closeness."

One of the biggest problems is finding time to be a wife and husband in the midst of the blended family. "We make the extra effort not to lose touch with each other. No matter how busy we are, we take a two- or three-day mini vacation every second or third month, sometimes to the beach, other times to the mountains. Just the two of us. Charlie is romantic. He brings me yellow roses each month. Starting in January he brings one rose. Then he adds another rose for each month. In early December he brings home a dozen yellow roses. He writes romantic messages on beautiful cards. He tells me he loves me each day. And he is getting better at telling me his feelings!" Charlie is a marvelous role model for husbands.

Family Crisis

"We faced a crisis when Monica turned 17 and decided to quit school, get a job and move out. We were in turmoil. Her mother was encouraging her to be independent. Monica left. But she promised Charlie she would continue going to high school at night. It was hard to let her go; however, she still continued to be part of the family unit, seeing us after she was on her own.

"When our oldest sons started their last year of high school, Charlie's company, forced by a slowdown in the economy, gave him a choice of losing his job or transferring to one of 10 major cities in the United States. We all loved the Northwest, our church and schools, sports, friends and our home. None of us wanted to leave. In fact, we all felt sick.

"Glum faced, we called a family meeting and sat down in a circle in the living room and wrote our votes on slips of paper. Our unanimous choice was Denver, Colorado. Charlie seemed to think that was a good location. Later he changed his mind. None of us wanted to live in the Los Angeles area. Charlie is a man of prayer and I felt led to support him in his choice.

"As a result of our decision, Clay, standing a good chance of receiving a substantial scholarship, and Mike, unwilling to leave the Northwest and his friends, decided to stay and finish school. We leased our house and with Bev and Willie moved to Los Angeles."

A blended family unit hurts when fragmented. "Breaking up the family was hard on *all* of us. We needed them and they needed us. It was so difficult being separated. I was in crisis. I've been fragmented too many times in my life.

"But Monica, now 22, calls often. She looks to us for acceptance. We're a sounding board for her; we don't give her advice. Charlie and I try to stay out of the parent mold and listen. The last time she came South, we both felt she has finally accepted me.

"It's incredibly hard being a stepparent! Our family is not without problems. Our little guy Willie is now 14. Recently he ran away from home and was gone two days. He experimented with drugs. His rebellion is painful for us. The older kids had a difficult time believing he had done that and they've been talking with him long distance.

"We just returned from a visit to the Northwest. Willie was dropped off at the airport by his mother. He exuded excitement. She allowed him to drive her new car all over the city. As she said good-bye, she shoved $50 into his hand for the birthdays she missed. Now he has even less understanding of our discipline, and is pushing his dad and I to the max! Recently he has been telling me he really misses his own mother. He then looks for my reaction. It hurts. I've been taking care of him since he was four.

"I continue to learn valuable lessons. It's better to give because you want to, not because you have to! I am working on being more accepting and not judging. The only person who can really change is me, and that's the person I have to keep working on.

"I pray about this, and through prayer I receive guidance. I pray about what to say and when to keep quiet. Prayer helps. I am thankful for the good times in our home. I've drawn closer to the Lord because of all the challenges in stepparenting. I've learned how to become a more loving person. I couldn't do it without the Lord."

Two families blending their past histories into making today and tomorrow meaningful and worthwhile is truly an achievement! Laurie and Charlie have demonstrated it is possible to maintain a good relationship amid the on-going rush of problems. Faith in God and their strong commitment to their marriage has been the rock on which they stand.

Many factors in merged families account for success or failure: The ages of the children, the blending of personalities and, most important, the emotional maturity and spiritual awareness of the stepparents.

These are success stories. Consider what Joe, a teenager, said about his stepfather. "My stepdad is really a terrific person. He doesn't spend his money foolishly, and he gives my mother things she's never had."

"I have special feelings toward my stepfather," Arnie, 16, emphasized. "I was 10 when he married my mom. I realize now that the Lord allowed the divorce to happen. At the time I didn't have a spiritual interpretation. But now I view my stepfather as my spiritual father, my teacher and counselor. My mom and stepfather both came to know the Lord at the time of their marriage, and they've both been growing tremendously. My stepfather is a gift from God."

Stepparenting is not always successful, but Christians can claim the blessing of God on their household. By living the Christian life we can plant seeds of kindness, patience, love and understanding, and they will grow.

Before You Remarry

Be positive and confident about your emotional stability, that you are at the right place in your life, having dealt with past issues, and aware of your needs, and feeling certain that you are ready to make a commitment to a new marriage. Hopefully you have known each other at least four seasons.

Begin preparing the children well in advance for the merger of the two families. Give them liberal assurances you are still their parent and will always love them. The children will feel better if the new stepparent spends special time with them. After the marriage, don't insist they are to call the stepparent Dad or Mom. Let it be their choice. Letting them know the stepparent does not replace their birth parent helps them feel more comfortable.

Discuss limit setting before you are married. Make it fair for each of the children, his and hers. Talk it over. Who will discipline whose children? If it doesn't seem fair, share your feelings and fears. Be aware of potential resentments the children may have. Everyone needs their own space; a separate area for each child is advisable if they can't have their own room.

Keeping in mind children do not like change will help you understand some of their unsettled behavior after the marriage. They may act out their insecurities and anger.

After You Remarry

If at all possible move into a different house or apartment. Then no one will be living in the shadow of a former spouse. Your new place becomes ours, instead of his or hers.

As a couple, devote time alone with each child. Help the children to be expressive. Listen to them. Search for feelings. Look for special interests and talents to encourage. Remember a child might not appear resentful, for children can bury emotions just as adults do. By being alert you may circumvent trouble.

Birthdays and holidays are built-in opportunities to start your own traditions. Discuss them well in advance so everyone will feel comfortable. Perhaps it's possible to incorporate ideas from each family. Try not to discount the children's former customs in an attempt to make everything new and *ours*. Holidays are difficult for children when all the parents and grandparents (sometimes there are three sets of grandparents) insist on seeing the children on the day of the holiday. Children usually don't enjoy being shuffled from place to place. Remember, Christmas is a season, not just one day. So if this is a problem, why not keep peace and celebrate the holiday on another day? Or one year celebrate at one house, the next year at another.

Don't allow previous spouses to negate or sabotage your life-style or interfere with the philosophy of your home. For example, they might buy toys or pets for a child that you feel are not age appropriate. Or a non-custodial parent might play a game, *woe is me.* The message being, feel sorry for me. I can't buy you such and such. Your mom or dad has means that I don't have. The child may then feel he/she doesn't deserve nice things, and therefore feels unworthy. Discuss potential problems before the fact with the children and the non-custodial parent. If you experience on-going conflict in this area, seek professional help. A former spouse's hostility may not evaporate when you remarry. Especially if he/she blames you for their unhappiness. Your happiness can be extremely threatening to an insecure, angry person if their life isn't going well. They may take their anger out on the children to get back at you. Be prepared to help your children through conflicting emotions. A child torn to feel sorry for an unhappy parent becomes even more fragmented. Help them to see parent problems are not children's problems.

If husbands and wives neglect to work on their marriage, this may lead to another failure. Keeping love well and alive requires creative energy. If you did loving things before you were married, don't stop now! Try not to let the hassles the kids are having interfere with your relationship. Work at keeping it fresh and clear. Get away by yourselves. Find events you both enjoy. The family will benefit from refreshed moms and dads.

Years from now your family members will look back and realize the support and love you gave them. They will enjoy a sense of family, even from a blended family.

PART V
Divorce and the Church

17

The Church Can Help
The Divorced

*"For your hardness of heart Moses allowed
you to divorce your wives, but from the
beginning it was not so."*
—*Matthew 19:8,* RSV

WHEN CHRISTIANS GET DIVORCED, often there is a spiritual battle going on. It is not unusual for many Christians to divorce the Church at the same time. Instead of looking to the Church for guidance, comfort and help when they end a marriage, they lose their spiritual moorings. They may feel unworthy because they failed at something so important as marriage. This is not always the fault of the individuals.

The Family as Presented by the Church

Oftentimes the Church is to blame for presenting a cozy Christian family as the norm for Christian living. They show a husband (who is working), a wife (who remains at home) and 2.4 children. Whenever the Church pictures this stereotypical ideal and promotes programs for the family only, those passing through the gates of divorce may feel uncomfortable in that tidy family-oriented church.

Furthermore, there are churches that heap burdens of guilt upon the divorced. They preach the Law instead of grace, ideals instead of reality. The shattered dream of the happy Christian home is infused with guilt and shame, because divorce is a *no-no* for Christians. Some Christians can't bring themselves to return to that kind of church and, in many cases, no longer attend at all.

Any church that emphasizes Bible exposition teaches people to know what God's Word says. With Scripture to back up the Church's position, divorcing Christians find themselves further alienated from God.

Some Bible-taught believers reason: If God does not accept divorce, how can God smile on the divorced? If God does not accept divorce, why go to His house? He will not pay attention to my worship because He doesn't care about me any longer. I have not obeyed God's will. I have broken my vows and therefore His will. I have incurred His wrath. I am living under the anger of God. "What therefore God has joined together, let no man put asunder" (Matt. 19:6, *RSV*), but we have put asunder!

Is There Room for Sinners?

Is it any wonder divorced Christians ask: Is there any place in the Church for the Christian sinner?

There is indeed. Jesus not only died for our sins, but He accepts sinners. In that case then, what can the Church do to minister to the people of divorce?

Fortunately, not every church focuses its ministry to the typical Christian family. There are churches across America that carry on vast singles ministries. They work with the disillusioned. They minister to the hurting. They restore the brokenhearted. They are aware of the pain, guilt, shame and spiritual conflicts of divorce. They offer counsel, help, fellowship and the renewal of faith for those who have been shattered and feel defeated by life experiences.

When a Christian husband and wife divorce, the tendency is for one of them to leave the church. The church now has the opportunity to minister to the remaining partner. The one who leaves may attend another church, but generally drops altogether.

Divorce Recovery

Some larger churches offer divorce recovery workshops, a unique experience for those who are hurting and facing the possible breakup of their family. In these workshops they meet other people who are also suffering, and that in itself can become the first step to healing.

A number of the churches give these workshops as all-day seminars, while others offer them over a six-to eight-week period. These sessions cover many important topics, many of which we have discussed in this book—the reality of divorce, emotions, problems with children, dealing with common pitfalls, making new choices and the questions of dating and remarriage.

The Church's obligation and privilege is to counsel and care for the wounded and to bring all of its resources together in an attempt to promote a possible reconciliation. The Church needs to do more than it is presently doing in the area of counseling for the troubled, and to become more aware and sensitive to the needs of the people. When people come to the Church for counsel, often it is too late. But whatever the situation, the Church must bring the gospel to the suffering and give help in the process of making people healthy and whole.

Amy was divorced after 23 years of marriage. Her children were in their late teens, ready to leave home; the oldest was off to college. Amy found herself in a precarious situation.

"We were both active in our church when we were married, and when we separated he stayed. But where could I go? You can't both attend the same small church when you're divorcing. Everybody knows everybody else. Well, almost. It's awkward and embarrassing, but where can you worship when you've been in the same church for many years? I've known some of those people for a long time! So did he. I was out. Nowhere to go. With all the other trauma I was experiencing from the divorce, I had to find a new church.

"So I wondered, where do I meet the kind of people I want to associate with? At bars? I've never been to those places. I'm not going to start now! The health club? I'm not into that either. The church ought to be a place to meet friends and to get support, but my church's door was closed because my former husband was there.

"If I want male companionship now, where do I find it? I work with 10 salesmen. Most of them are characters. I've got plenty of men around me, who are all crazy. Where do I search for companionship? You have to have something in common. People at work are just not enough. I'm looking for someone who has similar goals, hopes, attitudes and faith in Christ.

"I'd like to see a church group that includes kids as well. Mine were having problems. Where could they get help? They need other Christian kids who have similar problems. That's what the church ought to provide."

Recovery Programs

Heart Healers, an eight-week program offered three times a year at one church, is a variation of the divorce recovery workshop. This program is designed to help all kinds of people who have suffered from broken relationships—marriages, engagements, death. This organization helps people transcend the grief process and face emotions through open discussion, small groups and personal counsel. Ministers, marriage counselors, youth pastors and others speak on the many issues of divorce. During those weeks they have even seen reconciliations take place.

Lectures are followed by small groups led by trained discussion leaders, who will help five or six people face specific problems. The people in each group tend to help each other. They call between meetings to offer prayer and encouragement. These small support groups are the very heart of the program.

Heart Healers advertises through the newspapers and over radio, inviting people from the community to attend. By not limiting their meetings to church people, they have become part of an outreach ministry. Those who come from outside the church are offered Bible classes, as well as counsel. Young people are integrated into the youth activities of the church.

Many who have tried to find companionship through other avenues like bars, health clubs, single-parent groups and other organizations become dissatisfied and begin looking for more. This is when the Church's door needs to be open.

One pastor in Southern California has a picture of a waterfall in his office symbolizing the fact that the waterfall is always in transition and is always there. So is their ministry to singles. As people attend a meeting there they get touched by the caring, message and Spirit of God, even if they only come a few times. They are in transition and often don't know what they are doing or what they really want. But if they can stay with a healing church that offers the grace of God through people who care, seekers discover the power of the Lord through church fellowship and the ministry of compassion.

Another church has a couple who make themselves

available every Wednesday night to listen to anyone who wants to drop in and talk. Anyone can walk into the church's fireside room. They call their program Transition and Support.

The couple who have made themselves available have been through divorce themselves. If needed, they make referrals to pastors, psychologists, counselors or community services. Some come only once to Transition and Support, while others return week after week.

Some evenings no one shows up. On another night a mother whose teenage son is threatening suicide or a man in tears because his wife has left to live with another man come to the fireside room. This unique ministry has become a turning point in many lives!

Another church seeks mature Christians to work as advisors to singles. These Christians give credibility to the group and minister to their needs. They are part of the small care groups where individuals desiring fellowship enter and are accepted. Care groups study the Bible and pray for the 10 or 15 singles who belong. They also attend a monthly Sunday brunch and include outings in the park, a movie or a musical in their activities.

Groups for Singles

There are numerous single Christian parents who shy away from these groups. They are embarrassed to be part of the singles scene, but few churches offer opportunities for mixing couples with singles. Once part of a couple, now single, some Christians feel it's a step down to attend a church's singles group.

"My secretary felt so strange the first time she walked into a singles group," commented one pastor. "She used to be with couples. This was a tremendous transition for her. A comedown in her mind from traveling first-class (being married) to having to be a single again, and a divorced one at that. And if Christian adults can't face this easily, how do you suppose the kids feel?"

All hurting people, including parents and children, need the support of the Christian community. They need to experience the Body of Christ at work, healing, forgiving, redeeming, for that is the task of the Church of Christ. A true understanding of Scripture brings us to the grace of God in Christ: "For God so loved the world, that he gave his only begotten Son, that whosoever believeth in him should not perish, but have everlasting life" (John 3:16, *KJV*). Love is the heart of the good news. If people don't find grace and love (in the church), something is wrong! Christians believe in a redemptive gospel. The fact is that the Church has much to offer single-parent families that they will never find anywhere else. It is comfort— "Comfort ye, comfort ye my people, saith your God" (Isa. 40:1, *KJV*).

What brings most singles to a church group? Seeking a mate is a strong motivator. Ask any group of singles if they want to be remarried and you will almost always see every hand raised. Then ask them what they think of when they consider remarriage, and some confess fear, or fights, or even glutton for punishment. But they all want to be married!

The singles group in one church is called The Other Ones. The title conveys the other side of the tracks, not acceptable persons! Second-class citizens. Any church that transmits this type of message will further alienate people from Jesus Christ. This church needs to reevaluate its position. No one belongs on the other side of the tracks. At the foot of the cross, we are all equal. That is where we all meet our Saviour!

In 1 Corinthians 6 and 7 the apostle Paul discusses the advantages of being single. Consider the lives of the apostles, the saints who have devoted themselves to serve God in celibacy. Consider our Lord Jesus Christ Himself. When the discussion of marriage and divorce arose with the religious leaders, Jesus was firm about the will of God. The disciples were disturbed about His teaching. Maybe "It is not good to marry" (Matt. 19:10, *KJV*), they blurted out.

Jesus replied: "That is something which not everyone can accept, but only those for whom God has appointed it. For while some are incapable of marriage because they were born so, or were made so by men, there are others who have themselves renounced marriage for the sake of the kingdom of Heaven. Let those accept it who can" (Matt. 19:12, *NEB*).

Ministry for Single Parents

There is no shame in being single. Statistics indicate that almost 50 percent of the U.S. population over 18 is single.

Some pastors working with single parents see in them more courage, more growth than anywhere else in the Church. It's sink or swim for them. Crucial issues are at stake and in their need divorced singles find God, as they minister to one another. The ones who swim become strong swimmers indeed!

Many churches are including children in their ministries to single families. They plan films, barbecues, picnics and retreats for single parents and their children.

One church has camp outs for single-parent families. Camping is a fun and inexpensive way to have a good time. Campers are only required to bring sleeping bags and basic necessities. Everything else, including equipment, is provided.

Another church provides a unique program on Saturdays. Conceived and run by a group of single men, this program is known as Good Shepherds. Children of single moms are taken by these men to the mountains or the beach for a day. Recently mothers who have benefited from Good Shephards hosted a thank you. They took the men to a major league baseball game, with the children of course. A lot of good feelings have resulted from this ministry. A couple of marriages have even taken place.

Deacons and families from the mission committee of another church included single parents and their children on a trip to an orphanage in Mexico. This gave the children an opportunity to be with other children from single-parent families and to be involved in a rewarding project.

Another congregation is considering a recovery program expressly for children. When they plan a divorce recovery workshop, they expect to offer a simultaneous program for children of divorce.

Some churches are exploring the possibility of a special class for remarried couples with children. "These couples need help to face the unique problems of blended families and stepparenting," a pastor stated.

During a committee meeting discussing the need for this class, a recently remarried man confessed: "I'm near the edge of a second divorce and I need this class." Remarrieds don't consider their problems the same as those who have traditional families. Consequently they don't feel free to speak up in ordinary couples classes. But once they've been through the singles scene, they're far more open and aware. The pastor advising them is excited about the way in which these couples are able to come to grips with issues and how they relate to each other.

Sherry attended this planning meeting. She admitted: "In my first marriage I was afraid to say anything. Then I was divorced for five years. In this new marriage I'm afraid *not* to say anything."

"Ministering to children in a remarried situation is very important," offered one pastor. "It's difficult enough enduring a divorce, but sometimes it's worse being in a new family. The dynamics of stepparenting are overwhelming. We want to offer help."

Another idea that has been advanced by some churches is a *divorce prevention* workshop. Several singles attend a class of marrieds. They explain what happens when divorce occurs, how it affects the entire family. Singles could well share many of the ideas and problems discussed in this book, how moms, dads, kids and grandparents are touched by divorce. Perhaps as a result the married would put more effort into their relationships instead of proceeding to separate. What would happen if families read a book like this while experiencing a troubled marriage and begin to work more diligently at that relationship?

That's a recommendation for any church to try.

The Small Church

What if the church has limited resources? What if the church's membership is 200 to 300 and there aren't enough people for a singles group? What can the small church do?

Support and connect with a singles ministry of a larger church, said many pastors and singles we interviewed. The singles ministry requires a large number to attract others. Singles go where singles are. Instead of conducting a small group in a small church, it is best to provide an opportunity where ministry and counsel are available.

A pastor of a small church may be afraid to lose the few members he has to a larger church. He may even oppose someone attending a singles group at another church. But people who feel loyal to their own congregation return for worship and the responsibilities in their churches. Larger churches encourage people from smaller churches to participate in their singles groups and activities, but to worship in their own churches.

Smaller churches can include divorced people in leadership to integrate them into the life of the church. It is important to make single parents feel valuable. Smaller churches can band together to form an association for singles across denominational lines. Any church that has no more than five or six singles together will not succeed with a singles program unless it's to enjoy a small after-church brunch. Even that will surely help the lonely.

A church might consider searching for a couple who have experienced divorce to help establish a small group that meets weekly. By getting on a mailing list of a larger church, information would be available when divorce recovery workshops are being offered.

Many pastors feel it is necessary for the church to clearly define its position on divorce and remarriage. Some churches take a stance that is unpopular with the singles community and mute that position. But the true beliefs of the church seep through. If any church denies remarriage but offers a singles ministry, this acts as a contradiction.

"The churches who don't believe in remarriage don't have singles," quipped a pastor. "Their singles are treated as lesser Christians."

What is your church currently doing for singles? Can you see a need for a change in attitude? What can you as an individual do to help and care for those who are recovering from divorce?

18

The Benediction

"To every thing there is *a season,
and a time to every purpose
under the heaven."*
—*Ecclesiastes 3:1,* KJV

TOGETHER WE HAVE WITNESSED the impact of divorce and the shaking of our inner being. We have followed the stages, from hopelessness to hope, like the seasons through which we move.

In the fall, the leaves on an aspen change from green to gold etched with scarlet. The leaves whirl and dance in the wind. The heady triumphal scene of autumn! As the weather changes, chilling the earth, the dancing leaves one by one fall silently to the ground. Eventually the aspen is bare. Blackened scars, formed by broken limbs and branches from yesteryears, become visible as the tree, gray-white, stands vulnerable to the chilling cold of winter storms.

Cruel, harsh winter delivers its passing blows, but winter is transient. Another season arrives. Spring. The tree responds to warmth. New life stirs. Sap flows. Buds swell and branches burst into glory looking forward to even warmer days and summer. The aspen stretches heavenward, as though to say, praise you, thank you God for new life, new hope, new beauty, new joy (see Ps. 96:12).

The seasons of divorce follow a similar process. Once tender green shoots of love changed into broken forms. Dreams shattered left emotional scars. A hopeless marriage falls apart.

If only the fall, the season of heady liberation, could last forever! While it lingers there is a rushing from pain, escaping, running. Deep in the soul we know the whirling cannot go on, but it feels better than facing an empty apartment, or a home with children who want comfort, guidance, security. We become drained, empty, as though life, like water, has passed through our fingers and we have nothing to offer. If the denial of pain could last forever, the dancing would not have to end.

Winter comes. Formidable. Inevitable. The whirling ceases. Numbness sets in. The frozen face of despair appears. Other faces of winter knock at the door. Depression and anger. Though scarred and vulnerable, we discover winter's guests will leave if we don't take shelter in their grip for too long.

Before depression and anger can turn into the embalming frost of bitterness they will be ushered out the door.

There is a stirring in the soul. The awakening comes often at our lowest point. Spring is the turning! New life surges, and hope provides strength to face ourselves. The process of healing has begun. Tenderly. It is fragile, and there may be frequent setbacks. But the winter of divorce has ended! Spring will lead to the warmth of summer.

A new vision emerges from our shattered forms and broken dreams. God promises in His Word to meet us in our brokenness (see Psa. 51:17). He never leaves us nor forsakes us. This gives us great assurance and comfort!

Our merciful God does not punish us for our failures and mistakes. He redeems us and helps us back on our feet. He delights in helping us find our way again to live forgiven, fruitful and fulfilled lives.

In praise and thanksgiving let us turn to the *Lord of all Seasons*—with hope!

Suggested Reading

For Adults

Allen, Charles L. *When a Marriage Ends*. Old Tappan, NJ: Fleming H. Revell, 1985. Healing and compassionate counsel for dealing with the aftermath of divorce.

Berne, Eric. *What Do You Say After You Say Hello?* New York: Bantam Press, 1975. Contains insights into human behavior for the serious reader.

Colman, Barry. *Sex and the Single Christian*. Ventura, CA: Regal Books, 1985. Deals with various aspects of sexuality.

Efird, James M. *Marriage and Divorce: What the Bible Says*. Nashville, TN: Abingdon, 1985. Help in exploring the Bible's teachings, considering biblical culture and principles.

Gardner, R.A. *Psychotherapy with Children of Divorce*. New York: Aronson, 1975. Psychotherapeutic approaches to the resistant child.

Hosier, Helen K. *To Love Again: Remarriage for the Christian*. Nashville, TN: Abingdon, 1986. Comprehensive source of insight based on in-depth survey of divorced and remarried Christians.

Luepnitz, Deborah A. *Child Custody: A Study of Families*

After Divorce. Lexington, MA: Lexington Books, 1981.

Morgenbesser, Mel and Nadine Nehls. *Joint Custody: An Alternative for Divorcing Families.* Chicago: Nelson-Hall, 1981.

Pearson, Bud and Kathy. *Single Again: Remarrying for the Right Reasons.* Ventura, CA: Regal Books, 1985. Personal experiences regarding divorce and remarriage.

Roman, M. and W. Haddad. *The Disposable Parent: The Case for Joint Custody.* New York: Holt, Rinehart and Winston, 1975.

Smedes, Lewis B. *Forgive and Forget.* New York: Pocket Books, 1986. Forgiving is love's toughest work. A must for separated and divorced Christians.

Wallerstein, Judith S. and Joan B. Kelly. *Surviving the Break-up: How Children and Parents Cope with Divorce.* New York: Basic Books, 1980.

Ware, Ciji. *Sharing Parenthood After Divorce: An Enlightened Custody Guide for Mothers, Fathers and Kids.* New York: Viking Press, 1982.

Warshak, R.A. and J.W. Santrok. *Children and Divorce.* San Francisco: Jossey-Bass, 1981. The impact of divorce in father-custody and mother-custody homes; the child's perspective.

Warren, Neil Clark. *Make Anger Your Ally.* Garden City, NJ: Doubleday, 1983. Taming anger, the meanest emotion of them all.

For Parents and Children

Ed-U-Press, *Come Tell Me Right Away.* 1982. P.O. Box 583, Fayetteville, NY 10020.

Freeman, Lori. *It's My Body.* 1983. Seattle, WA: Parenting Press, 7750 31st Ave. NE, Seattle, WA 98115. For children 3-6 years.

Hutchinson, Barbara and Elizabeth Chevalier. *My Personal Safety Coloring Book.* 1982. Fridley Police Department, 6431 University Ave. NE, Fridley, MN 55432.

Sanford, Linda. *The Silent Children: A Parent's Guide to the Prevention of Child Sexual Abuse.* New York: McGraw Hill, 1982.

Stowell, Jo and Mary Dietzel. *My Very Own Book About Me,* 1983. Spokane Rape Crisis Center, Lutheran Social Services of Washington, 1226 N. Howard St., Spokane, WA 99201.

Wachter, Oraless. *No More Secrets for Me.* 1984. Little, Brown and Co. Distribution Center, 200 West St., Waltham, MA 02154.

The publishers do not necessarily endorse the entire contents of these publications.